PAUL
AND THE
GIANTS
OF
PHILOSOPHY

READING THE APOSTLE IN GRECO-ROMAN CONTEXT

EDITED BY

JOSEPH R. DODSON AND DAVID E. BRIONES

FOREWORD BY JOHN M. G. BARCLAY

ivp
Academic
An imprint of InterVarsity Press
Downers Grove, Illinois

InterVarsity Press
P.O. Box 1400, Downers Grove, IL 60515-1426
ivpress.com
email@ivpress.com

InterVarsity Press® is the book-publishing division of InterVarsity Christian Fellowship/USA®, a movement of students and faculty active on campus at hundreds of universities, colleges, and schools of nursing in the United States of America, and a member movement of the International Fellowship of Evangelical Students. For information about local and regional activities, visit intervarsity.org.

All Scripture quotations, unless otherwise indicated, are taken from The Holy Bible, New International Version®, NIV®. Copyright © 1973, 1978, 1984, 2011 by Biblica, Inc.™ Used by permission of Zondervan. All rights reserved worldwide. www.zondervan.com. The "NIV" and "New International Version" are trademarks registered in the United States Patent and Trademark Office by Biblica, Inc.™

Figure 1 is reproduced by permission from David E. Briones, Paul's Financial Policy: A Socio-Theological Approach. Library of New Testament Studies. London: T&T Clark, an imprint of Bloomsbury Publishing Plc, 2013.

Cover design and image composite: David Fassett
Interior design: Daniel van Loon
Images: Socrates statue: © araelf / iStock / Getty Images Plus
  the apostle Paul: © alexsol / iStock / Getty Images Plus

ISBN 978-0-8308-5228-4 (print)
ISBN 978-0-8308-7366-1 (digital)

Printed in the United States of America ∞

Library of Congress Cataloging-in-Publication Data

Names: Dodson, Joseph R., editor. | Briones, David E., editor.

Title: Paul and the giants of philosophy : reading the apostle in Greco-Roman context / edited by Joseph R. Dodson and David E. Briones.

Description: Downers Grove, Illinois : IVP Academic, an imprint of InterVarsity Press, [2019] | Includes bibliographical references and index.

Identifiers: LCCN 2019027274 (print) | LCCN 2019027275 (ebook) | ISBN 9780830852284 (paperback) | ISBN 9780830873661 (ebook)

Subjects: LCSH: Bible. Epistles of Paul—Criticism, interpretation, etc. | Philosophy and religion. | Philosophy, Ancient.

Classification: LCC BS2650.52 .P3648 2019 (print) | LCC BS2650.52 (ebook) | DDC 227/.06—dc23

LC record available at https://lccn.loc.gov/2019027274

LC ebook record available at https://lccn.loc.gov/2019027275

| P | 22 | 21 | 20 | 19 | 18 | 17 | 16 | 15 | 14 | 13 | 12 | 11 | 10 | 9 | 8 | 7 | 6 | 5 | 4 | 3 | 2 | 1 |
| Y | 39 | 38 | 37 | 36 | 35 | 34 | 33 | 32 | 31 | 30 | 29 | 28 | 27 | 26 | 25 | 24 | 23 | 22 | 21 | 20 | 19 |

For

HAILEY AIDA BRIONES

and

AIDAN PAUL DODSON

May enough never be too little,
and Christ always be more than enough.

CONTENTS

FOREWORD

JOHN M. G. BARCLAY

PAUL LOVED CONVERSATION. His letters continue conversations that he had begun with the new believers in his churches. In the course of those letters he often constructs imaginary conversations with quick-fire questions and answers to get to the heart of an issue. And behind and beyond those letters we can imagine Paul's innumerable conversations with people he encountered: colleagues, converts, Jews, Greeks, Romans, fellow travelers, fellow artisans, customers, shopkeepers, city magistrates, fellow prisoners, and many more besides. In the Acts of the Apostles, Luke pictures Paul in intense conversation wherever he went, sometimes with people who had received an extensive philosophical education. Of course, Paul was a Jew, but Judaism was not hermetically sealed: already for many centuries Jews had spoken Greek, read Greek, and thought in Greek, and even a Jewish Greek-language education would make pupils aware of the central topics and categories that shaped the late Hellenistic culture inhabited by everyone in Paul's day. Paul had learned to be "all things to all people" (1 Cor 9:22), finding common ground for conversation, culturally adjusting to his context, and adapting his language for different audiences. His mind was unusually supple and versatile, not least to ensure that the "good news" he announced really came across as "good."

The rich and diverse chapters in this volume create new and significant conversations for that extroverted and talkative apostle. We do not know how far Paul's education extended into direct literary engagement with the giants of Greek and early Roman philosophy, but that is not the point. The conversations created here do not presuppose that Paul had read Aristotle, Cicero, Epictetus, or Seneca: comparison can work very well without a genetic link. The purpose of these chapters is not to prove that Paul knew this or that philosophical idea (though it is certainly possible that he did). The purpose, rather, is to put Paul into dialogue with other people in his cultural context who thought just as deeply about many of the topics that mattered greatly to him. Every comparison requires some points of similarity to make it worthwhile, some common ground to make the conversation interesting. But what often emerges at the same time is an awareness of difference, and to think carefully about such differences is to expose the underlying assumptions and deep cultural narratives at play beneath the surface of the conversation. Why does Paul think what he does about suffering, friendship, slavery, communal support, or gifts? When we put him alongside others who thought about the same topics and who came out with sometimes similar and sometimes startlingly different conclusions, we get a better grasp of what shapes Paul's thought and why his mind works as it does. Just as we clarify our own ideas and understand our own assumptions better when we argue them through with someone else, so putting Paul into discussion with a variety of conversation partners helps bring to the surface things we had never realized before.

The authors of these chapters have all done firsthand, in-depth research on the topics they bring to our attention. At the same time, they wear their learning lightly, and draw us into their themes with a lightness of touch that makes these chapters easy to read. They, and the editors, are warmly to be thanked for leading us into this room full of such interesting and varied conversation. If, perhaps, one topic does not interest you greatly, I am sure another will. You will find yourself here introduced to authors and texts you may never have read; some, perhaps, you have not even heard about before. That is exciting, like travelling to a country you had never previously visited and getting your head around the different ways they think and speak.

I hope one of the effects of this volume is to lead more students to venture out into the great world of ancient philosophical and religious thought, with its sea of fascinating texts and its scintillating range of ideas. Perhaps after this you will pick up a translation of Epictetus, or read one of Seneca's letters or treatises, and see how engaging and interesting they are.

But at the same time, if you are anything like me, you will find here a lot of new insights on Paul that would never have occurred to you had you not seen Paul in this comparative perspective. Numerous times when reading these chapters I have found myself thinking, *I had never thought of that*, or *I had never seen it that way before*. Prepare to be surprised and intrigued, and from those reactions I hope you will be led to think more clearly, more deeply, and with greater comprehension about that incessant conversationalist, Paul, whose letters keep inviting us, across the centuries, to respond to his provocative discourse.

PREFACE

IN *PAUL AND THE FAITHFULNESS OF GOD*, N. T. Wright concludes that scholars need to pay more attention to Paul's subtle relationship with philosophy and to get past the tired notion that the apostle's interaction with philosophers was simply confrontational. While Paul's theology certainly collides in some measure with any philosophy that does not line up with his gospel, according to Wright, the apostle still didn't completely disregard or wholly reject the works of the philosophers—"as if one could throw all other books [but the Bible] away." What is needed then, Wright infers, is for more scholars to track, plot, and assess "the many lines and levels of Paul's engagement with his complex non-Jewish world."[1]

Since Wright published this book in 2013, a spate of scholars have done just that, and our aim here is to introduce you to some of their work. Our hope is that the following chapters will help you understand Scripture and Paul's theology better in order that your love for the Lord will abound in all knowledge and insight so that you may be better equipped to proclaim the gospel in our world today. Additionally, for those of you who plan on continuing in the academy, perhaps you will be inspired to join the endeavor to explore further (to track, plot, and assess) the apostle alongside the ancient giants of philosophy.

To help fulfill these goals, we have enlisted an international cast of diverse scholars to write about their comparative research on Paul and Greco-Roman philosophers for seminary and undergraduate students as well as interested laypeople. We have had so much fun with this project. This is especially due to our remarkable contributors

---

[1]N. T. Wright, *Paul and the Faithfulness of God* (Minneapolis: Fortress, 2013), 1:1407.

and to our team at IVP Academic. Our patient and kind editor, Anna Gissing, deserves our sincere thanks. We are also grateful for our former students Adam Jones, Nick Quinn, and Nathaniel Crofutt, who provided substantial administrative support that helped us get this to print.

Finally, Dave would like to dedicate this book to his little princess, Hailey Aida Briones. He prays that she grows into a godly woman who exhibits the Christian virtues of faith, hope, and love. I would like to dedicate this book to my son, Aidan Paul "Cheetoh" Dodson. I see God's fingerprints all over his life and pray that everything he touches will strike off something of the fire of divinity.

Joseph R. Dodson
Holy Cross Day
Denver

ABBREVIATIONS

BibInt	*Biblical Interpretation*
C&M	*Classica et Mediaevalia*
CCTC	Cambridge Classical Texts and Commentaries
CBQ	*Catholic Biblical Quarterly*
CurBR	*Currents in Biblical Research*
ExAud	*Ex Auditu*
HTR	*Harvard Theological Review*
ICC	International Critical Commentary
JBL	*Journal of Biblical Literature*
JRS	*Journal of Roman Studies*
JSNT	*Journal for the Study of the New Testament*
JSNTSup	Journal for the Study of the New Testament Supplement Series
LCL	Loeb Classical Library
LNTS	The Library of New Testament Studies
NICNT	New International Commentary on the New Testament
NIGTC	New International Greek Testament Commentary
NovTSup	Supplements to Novum Testamentum
NTS	*New Testament Studies*
SBJT	*The Southern Baptist Journal of Theology*
SBLDS	Society of Biblical Literature Dissertation Series
SBLTT	Society of Biblical Literature Texts and Translations
SNTW	Studies of the New Testament and Its World
THNTC	Two Horizons New Testament Commentary
TynBul	*Tyndale Bulletin*
WUNT	Wissenschaftliche Untersuchungen zum Neuen Testament
ZNW	*Zeitschrift für die neutestamentliche Wissenschaft und die Kunde der älteren Kirche*

PAUL AND THE GIANTS OF PHILOSOPHY

AN INTRODUCTION

DAVID E. BRIONES

EVERYONE HAS A CONTEXT. We don't exist in a vacuum. We all are necessarily shaped by the social, historical, political, religious, and philosophical factors at work in everyday life. Just think about how the 9/11 attack, the Boston Marathon bombing, and the Sandy Hook shooting have shaped the US as a nation. Though less horrific than these tragedies, philosophical ideas also have the power to mold us, whether we realize it or not. Consider how the individualism of Western society has misshapen the church. Individualistic philosophical ideas are like the billboards we pass on the freeway or hashtags we see on social media. "Be-YOU-tiful." "My mind. My body. My choice." "No Regrets." "Think different." "Image is everything." These pithy sayings are subtle yet powerful messages that can be traced back to deeper religious or philosophical reflection (many of which are repackaged from the ancient world). They carry the power to form or distort the way you think, feel, and act. Ideas shape us, whether they come from a song, a book, a classroom, a YouTube video, or a pulpit. At times, ideas shape us subtly, without being detected. But most times, they require our permission. We choose whether ideas will shape our thinking and living. This is a major part of our contextualized life. It is, as it were, a dialogue or a confrontation with ideas. What do we accept? What do we reject? Why? And how then should we live?

Paul's life was contextualized too. Only his context was first-century Greco-Roman society, a world filled with religious and philosophical ideas disseminated by philosophical giants such as Socrates, Plato, Aristotle, Cicero, Seneca, and Epictetus. Although all these titans didn't live during the first century AD, they left their mark on the ancient world. Their insights and explanations of humanity, life, death, community, and the divine were extended by their followers. Perhaps in contrast to our conception of modern philosophy, these ancient philosophers didn't promote ivory tower ideas. Theirs was an on-the-ground approach to life. Their philosophies were taught and caught. You heard them proclaimed and saw them explained. They were as much a doctrine as a way of life. Their teachers and followers were like living billboards, the kind Paul passed on Greco-Roman roads. "Eat, Drink, and Be Merry!" "Everything Is Permissible." "The Unexamined Life Is Not Worth Living." "Carpe Diem." This was the world in which Paul lived and ministered, learned and loved, taught and confronted. This was the place where he engaged with powerful ideas that shaped and misshaped people and where he sought out the minds, hearts, and lives of God's followers, seeking to secure their allegiance to the only true philosophy, the gospel of Jesus Christ. Paul's life and ministry was contextualized, and it is the Greco-Roman philosophical background that sets the stage for his dialogue with the giants of philosophy.

Now, Paul didn't really have a dialogue or discussion with any of the giants of philosophy discussed in this book. (Well, at least that we know of. There were letters purported to contain a correspondence between Paul and Seneca, but they have been falsified.) To be sure, Paul was aware of philosophical groups and their teachings, such as the Stoics and Epicureans (Acts 17:18-20), and he most likely had been exposed to other philosophical ideas based on parallels that one finds between his letters and the writings of the philosophers. But this can't lead us to assume that Paul read the works of the philosophers or that he had regular discussions with them in the marketplace. Some scholars make too much of these parallels between Paul and the philosophers—so much so that their work has been labeled "parallelomania" because they list an enormous amount of common words, phrases, and concepts found in Paul and the philosophers and then draw unfounded conclusions. Instead of focusing on superficial parallels, in the following pages we prefer to establish a dialogue between Paul and the giants of philosophy.

But what does it mean to put Paul in dialogue with these ancient philosophers when he never actually had a dialogue with them in the first place? It means that we create the dialogue. Each chapter in this book is like a host of a podcast who invites two very different guests to be interviewed. He or she will ask Paul and an ancient philosopher (or philosophers) questions on a specific topic in order to compare their perspectives. Similarly, our goal is to assess each side charitably yet critically, read their writings within their own philosophical or theological worldviews, and so create a dialogical comparison that sharpens or clarifies our understanding of what they taught and how they lived.

You may be asking yourself, "Why would I want to compare Paul with non-Christian philosophers?" That's a fair question. But a response is simple. Comparison brings clarity. In fact, we experience this comparative clarity all the time. When you ask your friends where they want to eat, you'll usually have several options to compare before a choice is made. When you think about which school or seminary to attend, you'll usually compare the pros and cons of each before making a final decision. We compare which route to take home, whether the interstate or the streets. Many other examples could be given.

The point is that comparison brings clarity. And yet, that doesn't mean comparison necessitates sameness. We don't want to be parallelomaniacs, scholars who go overboard cataloguing hundreds of superficial similarities. These scholars often assume that verbal or conceptual parallels between Paul and the philosophers means each understood the word, phrase, or concept in the exact same way— that they meant the same thing when they used the same words.

Obviously, that's not true. Anyone knows that you can use the same word but import a different meaning. Just have a conversation with your British friend about your "pants" and find out. Like any dialogue, the parties involved will agree on some things but disagree on others. Their thoughts will both converge and diverge, especially when we're dealing with two parties who have fundamental differences. Those who wish to ignore these fundamental differences assume that discovering parallels means we discover sameness. This is just bad historical work. It doesn't take much effort to see that Christianity clearly differs from pagan philosophy. And yet, the opposite extreme is also wrong. Many scholars assume Christianity's fundamental difference with ancient philosophers means they shouldn't be compared at all. The approach of this book lands in the middle of these two pendulum swings.

Comparison brings clarity, not absolute sameness or absolute difference. A comparison, for example, of Paul and Aristotle on the topic of ethics can't assume they had identical conclusions or that they worked within the same theological/philosophical framework. But neither can one naively assume that there is no overlap or similarity. Good historical, theological, and philosophical work should account for sameness as well as difference, doing justice to both.

This sort of critical juxtaposition helps sharpen our understanding of Paul and the philosophers. We realize that Epictetus's philosophical ideas, on certain levels, resonate with Paul's theology, and that Paul's theological ideas, on certain levels, resonate with Epictetus's philosophy. But these similar resonances can never be at the most fundamental level. Paul and Epictetus are *not* two peas in a pod. They neither believed in nor worshipped nor lived for the same God. Serious differences abound. But if we solely define them by their differences, then we'll miss out on the unique questions that emerge when we make comparisons—questions that sharpen and refine our understanding of Paul.

It's easy to believe a truth claim in isolation. People do it all the time. But when a person with a very different perspective disagrees with you, it forces you to know what you believe, why you believe it, and why you don't believe what they believe. The same can be said of comparisons. When a philosopher gives his perspective on the afterlife, and Paul gives an entirely different perspective, then we're led to ask higher-level questions. What exactly leads Plato to affirm his distinct view of the afterlife? What prevents Paul from promoting the same view? How do their broader philosophical or theological commitments play a role in their arguments? Comparative studies compel us to search the Scriptures assiduously, to examine the philosopher(s) diligently as well as charitably, and to achieve an informed conclusion on the matter. And that process is priceless.

We hope this volume gives you a glimpse into the comparative enterprise of Pauline studies. It has recently been a burgeoning enterprise among New Testament scholars. Several PhD dissertations have been published in the past ten to twenty years that compare Paul with another influential thinker in or around his first-century context. We just want to whet your appetite here. Each chapter is introductory rather than exhaustive. They will generally follow a dialogical pattern, comparing Paul with one or more giant of philosophy. Each perspective will be given before determining the points of similarity and difference. The goal will be to expose readers to the act of comparing, to illumine their understanding of Paul in his Greco-Roman philosophical context, and to introduce them to the distinct vantage point of non-Christian philosophers. At the end of each chapter, readers will find a list of primary and secondary sources. We encourage students to track down those sources for further study. Along with those sources, we have included discussion questions to provoke deeper engagement with the material covered. We hope that this initial foray into the comparative world of Pauline studies helps students see the value of comparing thought worlds, even if they're worlds apart.

While not every comparison in New Testament scholarship is helpful or insightful, our hope is that the many dialogues in this book will prove illuminating and beneficial. But the reader should note that they are intended to be a first word rather than the final word. Whether each chapter actually is an insightful first word on the matter will be up to the discretion of the reader, but that is at least our aim.

Allow me, then, to introduce the philosophical giants we will bring into conversation with the apostle Paul. Imagine a coffee shop with a rectangular table where the discussion will take place. The four sides of the rectangle represent four schools of thought. These "schools" were not formally established institutions, but a group of like-minded philosophers with an agreed leader. They were essentially ancient cliques or, perhaps a better comparison, philosophy clubs. These schools regularly met at certain locations in ancient Athens, which determined the name of their school. The Stoics met on the porch, that is *the Stoa* (Stoicism), the Epicureans in *the Garden* (Epicureanism), the Academy just outside the city walls in or among a grove of olive trees (Academics), and the philosophers who were "given to walking about" in the *Lyceum* (Peripatetics). They all agreed that there is a single correct view of reality, that true ethics is based on it, and that true logic will reveal it. But besides generally agreeing on those foundational principles, they parted ways in their specific teachings on physics, logic, and ethics. These four schools (like cliques or clubs) have their own distinct personalities and philosophical ideas. Each person at the discussion table belongs to one of these schools: Stoicism (Aratus, Epictetus, Seneca), Epicureanism (Philodemus), the Academy (Plato, Cicero, Plutarch), and the Peripatetics (Aristotle). Soon, Paul will pull up a chair and strike up a discussion with these philosophers. But before that takes place, let's survey who these philosophers are. We encourage you to reference this cast of characters as you make your way through the book.

Descriptions of Philosophers

Aratus (ca. 310–240 BC)	A Greek didactic poet. He wrote a hexameter poem called *Phenomena*, which became very popular in the Greco-Roman world. Paul quotes him in Acts 17.
Aristotle (383–322 BC)	Studied under Plato. Founded a philosophical school called "Peripatetic." One of the most influential philosophers among Christian theologians. His most relevant works are *Nicomachean Ethics*, *Eudemian Ethics*, *Rhetoric*, and *Politics*.
Cicero (106–43 BC)	A Roman politician who was a brilliant orator and well-educated in philosophy. Toward the end of his life, he penned a series of philosophical works focused on major topics in Greek philosophy. As an Academic skeptic, he argues both views on a matter but refrains from adopting either, which he considers the best option. Among his most important works are *On Final Ends*, *On the Republic*, *Tusculan Disputation*, and *On Duties*.
Epictetus (ca. AD 50–120)	Former slave turned Stoic philosopher. Studied under the Stoic Musonius Rufus. Arrian, his pupil, wrote down his teachings in four books (*Discourses*) and a handbook (*Enchiridion*). One of the most practically minded philosophers. He focuses primarily on ethics rather than theoretical argumentation.
Philodemus (ca. 110–40/35 BC)	An Epicurean philosopher. Many of his writings were excavated from a villa at Herculaneum that was destroyed by the well-known eruption of Mt. Vesuvius. Although fragmentary with stilted prose and therefore inaccessible to the armchair philosopher, his writings remain an important source of Epicurean views on a number of topics.
Plato (ca. 429–347 BC)	Studied under Socrates and taught Aristotle. Founded a school of philosophy in Athens called "the Academy." He was the first philosopher to promote philosophical views in dialogue and dialectical forms. Along with Aristotle, Platonic philosophy would greatly influence the Christian theological tradition and the wider Western world.
Plutarch (ca. AD 45–120)	Wrote many philosophical works in addition to essays and a work on the lives of great Greeks and Romans. Promoted a standpoint called "Middle Platonism." Although very critical of Stoicism and Epicureanism, his writings provide much insight on these two philosophical schools of thought.
Seneca (ca. 4 BC–AD 65)	Stoic philosopher. Tutor to the emperor Nero, who eventually forced Seneca to commit suicide. Like Epictetus, Seneca was very much focused on the practical benefits of philosophy. He wrote several philosophical essays and letters that present Stoic moral theory in a more accessible manner than do most philosophers.

1

"WHAT DOES NOT KILL ME MAKES ME STRONGER"

PAUL AND EPICTETUS ON SUFFERING

DOROTHEA H. BERTSCHMANN

NOBODY LIKES SUFFERING. Hardship, illness, and loss are things we try our best to avoid, perhaps more so than ever in our developed Western societies, where a lot of energy is invested in the "pursuit of happiness." But suffering will not go away. Are there ways to get at least something good out of it? Can suffering really make us stronger or make us better, like a bitter but wholesome medicine? In this chapter, I will look into the answers the apostle Paul and the Stoic Epictetus give to the question, "Can suffering be an instrument to turn us into more ethical people?"

EPICTETUS

Epictetus and his teaching. What is it that Epictetus's eager students wanted to learn? It was the pursuit of happiness, *eudaimonia*—except "happiness" is a very different concept for a Stoic than for us. It is best translated as "human flourishing," or becoming the best possible version of yourself. And this, in turn, happens when human beings live fully in accordance with their nature. But what is human nature? What singles out humans is that we are rational beings; we are able to live in a certain distance from the things happening to us; we can evaluate them and form a judgment. This is exactly what fascinates Epictetus. According to him, human beings are gifted with the rational faculty of *prohairesis*, literally, the faculty of "pre-choice," which can be translated as "volition." This faculty of *prohairesis* is like one big inner evaluation center. While our senses flood us constantly with external impressions, it is the job of the "rational" me to evaluate them properly and form true judgments.

Though this sounds straightforward enough, it is actually a difficult task that demands our full attention and involves a life-long process of practicing. Let's assume somebody offers you your dream job. Clearly this is a case for rejoicing. But no, says Epictetus, that amazing job is of no consequence for your happiness, rightly understood. There is no reason to decline the offer, but you should not rate it as something "good." It has to be classified as "indifferent." If you think that job is going to make you happy, you will strive and scramble for it and completely lose your inner peace. Worse, it is not in your power to get that job for sure. You are therefore placing your happiness in something outside of your control. This is the central problem.

Epictetus teaches that all external things, whether jobs, houses, wealth, fame, health, or relationships with our loved ones must be seen as "indifferent," and we must neither desire nor avoid them, because they are outside our control. Moreover, they do not affect the "real me" in the least bit, neither by our gaining them nor by our losing them. They do nothing for our happiness. Even your own body belongs to the externals, over which you have no control. So what *does* contribute to one's happiness? According to Epictetus, being a virtuous person equals being a happy person. This does not mean, however, that you feel good about yourself after carrying heavy shopping bags for an old lady.

When Epictetus speaks about ethical goodness he speaks about "virtues," which in Greek simply means "excellence." The person who realizes moral excellence, who is the best possible "me," is truly flourishing and in that sense happy. At the most basic level, this means once again living in harmony with your human rational nature. It means that the *prohairesis* watches over the sensual impressions and the gut reactions that come with them: Somebody punched you? It does not matter. Somebody praised you? It does not matter. You won the lottery? Irrelevant. You lost your home? Of no consequence to your flourishing. In a further sense *prohairesis* means growing virtues, permanent ethical traits such as modesty, kindness, and patience. And this growth as a virtuous person is the only thing that matters. This is what nobody can take from you, no matter the circumstances. If you desire these good things, nobody can hinder you from achieving them. You are a completely free person. This is ultimately the payoff for the rational human being: you are in complete control over yourself. You live in harmony with nature and ultimately with God. You are calm, serene, fearless, and completely at peace.

Epictetus and suffering. It is one thing to discipline your gut reaction after somebody offers you a job or asks you to marry them. It is quite another thing to remain calm and peaceful when your child or loved one is dying or when your colleague is a bully. But this is exactly what a person should aspire for, according to Epictetus. It is important to see that joyful events have to be scrutinized and judged by the *prohairesis* just as much as painful ones. But obviously the proverbial "Stoical attitude" is more impressive in dire circumstances. What does Epictetus make of what we call "suffering"? Does he see it as an instrument or as some kind of bitter medicine to help us become a stronger, better person?

Epictetus was certainly familiar with all sorts of hardships. He experienced the powerlessness of slavery and even after gaining his freedom he lived a frugal life. He was familiar with the fickle nature of those in power, as he was himself banned from Rome by the emperor Domitian. He also often mentions the dangers of travelling. And he talks about the terrible punishments inflicted by those in authority as well as of the agony of a raging fever.

There is one figure of thinking, which we find repeatedly in Epictetus, when he deals with suffering. This is the metaphor of the athlete. Epictetus often compares life to an athletic struggle, an *agōn*. Hardship and sufferings play the part of a fellow wrestler:

> It is difficulties that show what men are. Consequently, when a diffi-
> culty befalls, remember that God, like a physical trainer, has matched
> you with a rugged young man. What for? Someone says, So that you
> may become an Olympic victor; but that cannot be done without
> sweat. To my way of thinking no one has got a finer difficulty than the
> one which you have got, if only you are willing to make use of it as an
> athlete makes use of a young man to wrestle with. (*Disc.* 1.14.1-2)

In this struggle the athletes sweat, roll in sawdust, keep strict diets,
and endure painful massages (*Disc.* 3.5.3-5; 3.22.52). The active and
strained language is striking and seems to be at odds with the Stoical
calm. It sounds very much like the maxim "no pain, no gain."

But are sufferings needed to bring out the best in people? If we look
closely again at the quote above, we see that this is not the case. The
sweating, exercising, and fasting are not symbols for external hardships; they are metaphors for the life-long exercising of one's rational
judgment. It is not the painful loss or the fearful storm that brings out
the best in me. Quite the contrary, they have the dangerous potential
of bringing out the worst in me, making me react with spontaneous
grief or fear, which betrays my true "rational me"! Hardships and
awful circumstances have no meaning in and by themselves. But in
order to get to this point, the aspiring Stoic has to exercise her *prohairesis* regularly. She must review and judge external impressions
with the greatest discipline—a discipline not unlike that of an athlete
who wants to win the Olympic Games. What is crucial is this mental
exercise, which can feel like a strenuous effort and an arduous training.
This mental struggle is, however, only one side of the coin, of which
the other side is perfect calm:

> The man who exercises himself against such external impressions is
> the true athlete in training. Hold, unhappy man; be not swept along
> with your impressions! Great is the struggle, divine the task; the prize
> is a kingdom, freedom, serenity, peace. (*Disc.* 2.18.27-28)

In a way, the aspiring philosopher has to come to the point of understanding that suffering is nothing at all. Epictetus very tellingly
avoids the Greek word for suffering, *paschein*, which implies passivity

and powerlessness. Instead, he chooses words that can be synonymous for hardship and circumstances. The true Stoic does not suffer; he does not let hardship get to him. What we call suffering is really just a particular circumstance, which can be used as an opportunity for growth, just as the athlete uses weights to grow muscles. But there is more to it than simply growing one's "best me."

Epictetus often speaks about the "great day," when the athletes will finally run into the arena, cheered on by the crowds, and show what they are made of. The well-trained philosopher is also "showing off" his virtuous muscles for the benefit of others. He is a living evidence for the rationality of human beings, and he is a living witness for the goodness of God, who made people exactly that way (cf. *Disc.* 3.24.114).

For Epictetus, the ultimate contest is death, and the ultimate Stoic virtue is to be able to die without fear. His great champion in that respect is Socrates, who went to his death in complete calm. Exercising your rational judgments in daily hardship is to exercise for the time when you will be summoned to stay strong through dramatic hardship or death in order to witness to God. By learning how to live well you are practicing how to die well. Epictetus knows of no hope of an afterlife. But he insists that death is just as indifferent as getting or losing your dream job. It is, after all, just your body that is affected by it.

PAUL

Paul and suffering. Paul has a very different worldview from Epictetus. He does not preach the pursuit of happiness, understood as actualizing the true, rational "me," but he preaches salvation for all who believe (Rom 1:16). This salvation rescues from sin and its consequences, and it establishes a person in a new context as being "in Christ." In the power of the Spirit, such a person will not fail to flourish ethically as well. It has often been pointed out that Paul's catalogues of good and bad attitudes can be easily compared to philosophical lists of virtues and vices (e.g., Gal 5:16-26). But how might Paul connect suffering and ethical goodness? In order to answer this question, we must first examine Paul's attitude toward suffering in general.

Paul has, broadly speaking, two ways to refer to suffering. One frequent instance is when he narrates his own sufferings in an apologetic context. This occurs most prominently in his letters to the Corinthians such as in 2 Corinthians 11:23-33, where Paul lists all sorts of troubles: imprisonment, floggings, beatings, shipwreck, dangerous journeys, thirst, hunger, lack of clothing (see also 1 Cor 4:9-13 and 2 Cor 6:4-10). Paul refers to very similar things as Epictetus, but unlike the Stoic philosopher, Paul claims that he has undergone all these sufferings in the service of Christ, either as direct persecution or as hardships related to his mission as the apostle to the Gentiles.

In a paradoxical move Paul "boasts" in his sufferings and the weakness they caused him—not because he was man enough to endure them all, but because, for Paul, salvation is closely tied to the cross, and it is not surprising if the apostle of the crucified Lord carries "the death of Jesus" in his body (2 Cor 4:10, cf. Gal 6:17 and 2 Cor 1:5). Paul develops these thoughts under pressure to defend himself, but he strikes a much more nonpolemical and intimate note in other places. In fact, when Paul is at his weakest, God's grace is most fully experienced, he says in 2 Corinthians 12:10: "For whenever I am weak, then I am strong."[1] Moreover, in his letter to the Philippians, Paul muses that he wants to know "the sharing of his sufferings" and become conformed to Christ's death, surrounded by the power and hope of resurrection (Phil 3:10). Paul then accepts sufferings as an intrinsic part of his ministry and even as an apt expression of his message. If anything, affliction deepens his communion with Christ.

But does this mean that suffering is good for something? Will suffering bring people closer to salvation?

This brings us to the second category of Paul's remarks on suffering, which deals with his converts. When Paul speaks about the sufferings the believers share with him, his tone is less polemical and more encouraging. He assures the Philippians, for instance, that they should understand suffering for Christ as a gift (Phil 1:29). Still, Paul is also tangibly nervous in places. He knows full well that suffering for the

---

[1] All Bible quotations in this chapter are taken from the NRSV.

sake of the gospel can be unsettling and disturbing for his converts—after all they have responded to a message of salvation!

In 1 Thessalonians, Paul urges the young church not to be "shaken by these persecutions" (1 Thess 3:3) because afflictions have always been part of the Christian experience right from the beginning (1 Thess 1:6). Suffering was predicted (1 Thess 3:4) and is the shared fate of Christians elsewhere (1 Thess 2:14). The word Paul frequently uses is *thlipsis*, which has the connotation of "pressure" and "closing in." Paul knows that his young converts might well give in under the social and perhaps economic pressure they experience. He does not hail suffering as something good, but he sees it as an inevitable experience in a fallen and dark world. Although this present age is marked for destruction, it lashes out one last time against God's elect. In Philippians 1:28 Paul writes, "for them [the unbelieving outsiders] this is evidence of their destruction, but of your salvation." When Paul speaks like this he shares in a widespread apocalyptic worldview, which sees suffering as marking out the elect. Their sufferings, though intense, are just temporary (2 Cor 4:17), leading the way to a new quality of life, similar to the labor pains heralding a new life (1 Thess 5:3). Sufferings then, far from annulling the promise of salvation, are the sufferings of the righteous elect and will soon end.

But could they actually be the instrument or the "medicine" that makes us stronger, better people? There is only one passage in Paul where he explicitly connects suffering with what Epictetus would view as virtues. To this we turn now.

Suffering and virtues: Romans 5:3-5. Paul forms a kind of a chain in this passage, where the last element of a sentence is the first element of the next. This well-known rhetorical device in the first century makes for a very dense text. It reads as follows:

> We boast in our tribulations [*thlipseis*], knowing that tribulation works endurance, endurance character [literally, "approvedness"], character, hope. But hope does not bring to shame, because the love of God has been poured out into our hearts through the Holy Spirit, which has been given to us. (author's trans.)

In Romans 5, Paul has begun to unfold how, in Christ, sin's reign of death and condemnation is over so that peace with God and the "hope of sharing the glory of God" (Rom 5:2) abound instead. While human boasting was completely forbidden in earlier parts of Romans (e.g., Rom 3:27), believers now rightly boast in this hope. At this stage, Paul seems to anticipate a critical interlocutor saying: "Yeah, great. But what about suffering?" because he immediately adds the puzzling phrase about boasting in one's sufferings.

The reason for this is that sufferings (or "pressures," the word is *thlipseis* again) produce patience, or rather endurance. The Greek word for endurance, *hypomonē*, can be translated as "remaining under." The Roman believers show patience by remaining under their sufferings, despite the temptation to deny their faith and get rid of persecution and suffering, or more quietly to discard their faith out of disappointment. Paul does not tell us what tribulations he has in mind or how exactly they produce endurance. Endurance is most likely not something automatic, but involves human activity and effort. Paul here essentially says in an encouraging tone: "Let's brag about those sufferings because they bring out the best in you, namely steadfast endurance." Those who stand firm, in turn, will show themselves as "approved." Paul might have metaphors of the fire in mind, which shows precious metal to be "true." The word *dokimazō*, which means both "testing" and "approving," is sometimes used in these contexts (cf. Prov 17:3; Heb 12:5-11; Jas 1:12; 1 Pet 1:7). But is this fire testing or also refining? The way Paul uses the word group elsewhere suggests that he has in view a test and its subsequent seal of approval rather than a process of refining (cf. Paul's use of *dokimazō* in 2 Cor 8). Suffering is a "stress test," if you like, which reveals whether you are genuine or not. And if you know that you are suffering as a genuine believer, then you have a good basis for hope. This is the hope of the righteous, who must endure tribulations, but will eventually be vindicated and rewarded. (Paul has a similar worldview to that of Jewish martyr theology.)

Paul could leave it here. He has shown that the pressure of suffering is bound to bring out the best in the believers and subsequently assures them of their quality and rightful hope. But there is yet a much deeper reason for hope. And this reason is God's love, which he has shown in Christ and which he has poured into the very hearts of believers. Immediately after our text Paul makes it clear that God proves his love for us in that while we were still sinners Christ died for us (Rom 5:8). God's present love is firmly established in God's past deeds. This is the basis for unfailing hope, which is more than a vague optimism. In the present, God's love has been poured out into the hearts of believers, as God's gift, together with his Spirit. God's love literally reaches the innermost part of believers and becomes a part of them.

So there is indeed something like a chain reaction, in which suffering brings out the best in believers, namely, endurance, which in turn shows them to be genuine and therefore to have a good claim to hope. But this chain reaction of human responses to sufferings is held within a much bigger picture of divine love. It is this love alone that makes the "hope of glory" an assured reality for believers. And it is this love that makes endurance a worthwhile project for them.

We can see that Paul does not think that sufferings are God's bitter but wholesome medicine prescribed to make the believers grow into stronger, better people. This is astonishing, because in Paul's world there *was* a concept that made sense of suffering along these lines, namely that suffering was God's fatherly discipline, meant to restrain and correct his children (Heb 12:3-11). But Paul does not go there. The sufferings that believers sigh and weep about are neither the penalty of a stern judge nor the benevolent discipline of a strict father. They are simply there, as part of a chaotic world, turned against God's beloved. But though they are not good in themselves, God has already pulled them firmly under his salvific goal.

Conclusion: Paul and Epictetus on Suffering

Sufferings are not needed for ethical growth, neither for Paul nor for Epictetus. Quite the contrary, painful and harsh circumstances might tempt you to become less than human. They can tempt you to leave behind the truth of who you really are. In Epictetus's case, the deepest truth about the human condition is that human beings are rational and therefore equipped to be free. To counter this danger, Epictetus prescribes a very clear and life-long program of training your rational faculties. This can be an arduous and demanding task, but its reward is serenity, peace, and freedom. The goal is for me to realize that what we call suffering is really nothing, as far as my flourishing is concerned.

In Paul's case, the deepest truth about human beings in Christ is that they are loved by God and therefore resourced with undying hope. Paul is less systematic than Epictetus in his reflections on how to counter suffering. A measure of patient endurance and a subsequent increase of "provedness" and hope are part of the overall strategy. But this is held and empowered by the deepest reality of God's love, which lends substance to hope. Sufferings are very real in Paul's world, but they have lost their sting and power by being dwarfed by hope.

Epictetus's confidence is rooted in God's gift of the *prohairesis* given to humanity. Paul's confidence is rooted in God's love, which in the past was revealed in the sending of God's Son and which in the present is part of the believer's innermost person through the gift of the Spirit. Epictetus teaches spiritual self-sufficiency sponsored by God; Paul speaks of the divine restructuring of the self in a relationship of love, trust, and hope.

For both of these fascinating and deep thinkers, sufferings, though not a direct medicine, have the potential to activate one's "true me." What was out to warp and destroy your humanity eventually has to serve the goal of making you more human. No wonder both thinkers sound a note of ringing confidence: "Bring it on," says Epictetus, "bring on any hardship, and the good person will turn it into gold" (*Disc.* 2.2.35; 3.20.12).

And "this is the only contest into which the good man enters—namely, one that is concerned with the things that belong in the province of the moral purpose. How, then, can he help but be invincible?" (*Disc.* 3.6.7).

Paul, on the other hand, asks rhetorically whether there is anything in the wide world, including death and life, for that matter, that might separate us from the love of God. The only fitting response is a high note of praise: "We are more than conquerors through him who loved us" (Rom 8:37).

SIMILARITIES AND DIFFERENCES

Table 1.1. Similarities and differences

Epictetus	Paul
Sufferings are not needed for ethical growth.	Sufferings are not needed for ethical growth.
Sufferings can tempt a person to leave their rational judgment behind.	Sufferings, especially persecution, can tempt a Christian to become weary in their faith or even leave it.
For the aspiring philosopher, sufferings are an opportunity to exercise and strengthen one's rational judgment.	Sufferings are an opportunity for "boasting," because they will produce endurance and ultimately hope in the lives of believers.
This training can feel like arduous exercising at times but leads to complete calm.	Suffering must be taken on in patient endurance, which will lead to an increase of hope.
There is no suffering for a philosophical person. External circumstances cannot affect her in the core of her being.	Sufferings are real and affect the believer. They are not negated, but relativized in the hope of glory, where suffering will be overcome for good.
The philosopher trains to ultimately show calm in the face of death. This will be his greatest witness to God, who created him as a rational being.	God has given a very solid foundation to hope by showing his love in the past in Christ's death for them. This love dwells in the hearts of the believers and undergirds and empowers all their efforts to endure and hope.

FOR FURTHER READING

Primary Sources

Epictetus. *The Discourses as reported by Arrian, the Manual, and Fragments, with an English translation.* Translated by W. A. Oldfather. LCL. London: Heinemann, 1926–1928.

———. *Enchiridion.* Translated by George Long. Dover Thrift Editions. New York: Dover Publications, 2004.

Secondary Sources

Barclay, John M. G. "Security and Self-Sufficiency: A Comparison of Paul and Epictetus." *ExAud* 24 (2008): 60-72.

Beker, J. C. *Suffering and Hope: The Biblical Vision and the Human Predicament.* Grand Rapids: Eerdmans, 1987.

Eastman, Susan Grove. *Paul and the Person: Reframing Paul's Anthropology.* Grand Rapids: Eerdmans, 2017.

Engberg-Pedersen, Troels. "Paul, Virtues and Vices." In *Paul in the Greco-Roman World*, edited by J. Paul Sampley, 608-33. Harrisburg, PA: Trinity Press, 2003.

Harvey, A. E. *Renewal through Suffering: A Study of 2 Corinthians.* SNTW. Edinburgh: T&T Clark, 1996.

Jervis, L. A. *At the Heart of the Gospel: Suffering in the Earliest Christian Message.* Grand Rapids: Eerdmans, 2007.

Long, A. A. *Epictetus: A Stoic and Socratic Guide to Life.* Oxford: Oxford University Press, 2002.

Rowe, K. *One True Life: The Stoics and Early Christians as Rival Traditions.* New Haven, CT: Yale University Press, 2016.

Sauvé Meyer, Susan. *Ancient Ethics: A Critical Introduction.* New York: Routledge, 2008.

Tabb, B. J. *Suffering in Ancient Worldview. Luke, Seneca and 4 Maccabees in Dialogue.* London: T&T Clark, 2017.

DISCUSSION QUESTIONS

1. Does Epictetus's concept of *prohairesis* have a role in the life of the Christian?

2. What are the similarities and differences between the way Paul and Epictetus view death and virtues?

3. In what ways does Paul's confidence in the love of God improve upon Epictetus's concept of *prohairesis*?

4. For Paul and Epictetus, how is God involved in suffering?

2

THERAPY SESSION

PAUL AND PHILODEMUS ON THERAPY FOR THE WEAK

JUSTIN REID ALLISON

EPICURUS ONCE WROTE: "Let no one either delay philosophizing when young, or weary of philosophizing when old. For no one is under-age or over-age for health of the soul."[1] Health of the soul was a perennial concern for ancient Greek and Roman philosophers. Without it, there could be no flourishing human life. Particularly since Plato, philosophers competed to show that their philosophy offered the best treatment for the soul. By Paul's day, centuries-old philosophical traditions led immature students out of their emotional and mental illnesses toward health.

Throughout Paul's letters one notices a similar concern to counter destructive ways of living and to promote growth in those who believed the gospel. Faith in God involved radical personal transformation with respect to behavior, desires, conceptions of the divine, conceptions of self and others, religious allegiance, and social belonging (see Rom 6; 1 Cor 6:9-11; 12:2; Gal 2:20; Col 3:5-11). The decisive moment of transformation had already happened in coming to faith, and yet this transformation remained an ongoing battle against sin and the powers of darkness, against evil desires, emotions, and errant thoughts (e.g., 1 Cor 3:1-4; 10:1-22; Gal 5:16-21). To his "children" in Galatia, Paul wrote, "I am again in the pains of childbirth until

---

[1]Epicurus, *Letter to Menoeceus* 122, trans. A. A. Long and D. N. Sedley, in *The Hellenistic Philosophers* (Cambridge: Cambridge University Press, 1987), 1:154.

Christ is formed in you" (Gal 4:19).[2] Paul urged the Corinthian "infants in Christ" (1 Cor 3:1) not to reason like children, but instead to reason like "adults" (1 Cor 14:20). Paul repeatedly called believers to "build one another up" as they gathered in worship (Rom 14–15; 1 Cor 12–14; 1 Thess 5:11-22).

Philosophers of Paul's day routinely discussed how to adapt treatment of the soul to the needs of diverse patients. This was especially the case for students who were "weak," whose moral sickness complicated the therapeutic process by making them particularly vulnerable to harm. Similarly, in 1 Corinthians 8:1–11:1, Paul attended to believers who were "weak" and needed "building up" in comparison to others who did not share their vulnerability. At first glance, Paul's pastoral concern seems analogous to that of philosophers engaged in therapy for the "weak."

In light of this shared concern for the weak, we pursue two main questions in this chapter: First, how do Paul's directives to build up the weak in 1 Corinthians 8:1–11:1 compare to similar guidance given by an ancient philosopher? Second, how does this comparison enrich our understanding of Paul's vision for building up the weak?

The central purpose of this comparison is to view Paul's vision for building up the weak from a fresh, enriching vantage point. The perspective gained by this comparison is fruitful for contemporary Christian thinking about "building up the weak" (e.g., one might consider how Paul's discussion informs the consumption of alcohol in circles of American evangelical Christianity or ancestor worship in Chinese Christianity). Yet contemporary application is not the main focus of the chapter.

We will compare 1 Corinthians 8:1–11:1 to key passages of a treatise entitled *On Frank Criticism* (*PHerc.* 1471) written by the Epicurean philosopher Philodemus. This treatise is particularly useful for two reasons. First, Philodemus discusses at length how to care for weak students. Second, he emphasizes that all members of a philosophical

---

[2]All translations of biblical texts come from the NIV unless otherwise indicated.

community should take part in caring for one another, much like Paul emphasizes in 1 Corinthians 8:1–11:1. Thus, the comparison brings together two thinkers in historical and cultural proximity to one another who were concerned with offering guidance regarding similar issues in their respective communities.

Like Philodemus's other philosophical texts, *On Frank Criticism* (hereafter *OFC*) belongs to the only library from the ancient world that still exists, which Mount Vesuvius preserved when it erupted over the Bay of Naples in AD 79. The charred text of *OFC* is fragmentary, and the remaining legible portions often lack a clear context (citations below refer to fragment or column number). This work offers discussion upon the use of "frank criticism" or "frank speech" in Epicurean friendship to help others grow toward health of the soul and the best life.

In what follows, our first step is to gain an understanding of Philodemus's perspective on treating the weak. Our second step, moving back to Paul, is to identify important similarities and differences between the two, and then to sketch Paul's strategy to build up the weak with the help of our enriched perspective from comparison with Philodemus.

PHILODEMUS ON THERAPY FOR THE WEAK

To understand Philodemus's view of therapy, we need to understand the Epicurean analysis of the human problem and its solution through conversion to Epicurean philosophy. The best life was the most pleasurable life, according to the Epicureans. Contrary to common misconceptions, Epicureans were not indiscriminate hedonists. Epicureans thought that pleasure had limits, and that the greatest pleasure came from *ataraxia*, the complete absence of pain. According to their doctrine, the human problem is the problem of pain: all suffer from varied forms of pain caused by erroneous beliefs, unlimited desires, out of control emotions, or harmful behavior. They believed that over time our souls develop hardened dispositions toward false thinking, and thus toward causing pain to ourselves and others.

Epicurus offered a "fourfold cure" for pain: "(1) God presents no fears, (2) death presents no worries. And while (3) good is readily attainable, (4) evil is readily endurable."[3] This cure was central to Epicurean therapy; the entire philosophical system elaborated and supported its claims. Death is not to be feared, because you will not be alive to experience it, as there is no afterlife. When you die, your soul's atoms dissipate and you cease to exist. There is nothing to fear from the gods because they do not involve themselves with the human world.

Achieving the most pleasurable life was not just a matter of memorizing Epicurean beliefs. It involved the arduous transformation of one's psychological dispositions into virtuous, healthy dispositions to reason correctly, feel emotions properly, pursue desires wisely, and so forth. This transformation occurred most naturally with the constant help of friends committed to the Epicurean life. With this framework in mind, we may survey Philodemus's discussion of therapy via frank criticism, especially for weak students.

Frank criticism (*parrēsia*) is the use of philosophical persuasion to help another identify and eliminate causes of pain in one's thinking, feeling, desiring, and so forth (see *OFC* col. 9a; fr. 78).[4] Frank criticism was a primary means by which Epicureans delivered the cure of their philosophy. All frank criticism should fit the needs of the particular individual and his or her character. Usually, frank criticism involved a mixture of praise and censure alongside concrete instruction (discussed throughout *OFC*; see fr. 7; 10; col. 21a-24b).

Treating others through frank criticism required personal maturity in the Epicurean life. Philodemus assumed that more mature persons generally treated the less mature, for the immature did not have the capacity to treat themselves. Teachers bore the greatest responsibility

---

[3]Translation from Long and Sedley, *The Hellenistic Philosophers*, 1:156. This is a form of the cure cited by Philodemus in *PHerc.* 1005 col. 5 (numbered according to A. Angeli's critical edition: A. Angeli, *Filodemo: Agli Amici di Scuola*, La Scuola di Epicuro 7 [Naples: Bibliopolis, 1988]).

[4]Philodemus describes the use of frank speech in various ways: "rebuke" (Philodemus, *On Anger* col. 19), "correct" (*On Anger* col. 19), "admonish" (*OFC* fr. 36), "treat" (*OFC* fr. 79), and "save" (*OFC* fr. 36).

for the less mature, but students shared this responsibility as they became mature enough to do so (fr. 36; 79; Philodemus, *On Anger* col. 19). Ideally, friends regularly "saved one another" from painful vices via the reciprocal exercise of frank criticism (fr. 36). However, frank criticism could often go haywire, and Philodemus discusses at length the problems that inevitably arise, generally caused by immaturity in the giver or recipient.

The ideal recipient of criticism sought out help, responded approvingly to correction, and took steps forward in his progress toward maturity (see, e.g., fr. 44; 49; col. 1b-2a; 3b; 10b). Success in frank criticism thus required the active involvement of both the critic and the recipient, as well as an amiable relationship between the two.

"Weak" students were those who were immature, particularly those vulnerable to harm and who struggled to improve with treatment. They may have been unstable in their commitment to philosophy. Some may also have been "tender" (fr. 7), in that they needed a softer touch because they would crumple under pressure from harsh criticism. Fragment 59 describes them:

> but there are times when he [the immature student] will even shun philosophy, and perhaps will even hate the wise man, and sometimes he will submit, but will not be benefitted, although he [the teacher] has supposed that he will be benefitted. And these things will occur, I say, for many reasons. For since they are either weak or have become incurable because of frankness . . .[5]

For weak students, Philodemus championed a loving, adaptive approach. This approach involved, for example: forgiveness of minor faults (fr. 4; 20; 35), use of kind names like "dearest" and "sweetest" (fr. 14), refusal to mention the recipient's lack of progress (fr. 33), refusal to criticize every fault of the recipient at once (fr. 70; 78/80N), praise of the recipient's good qualities, and encouragement to act in accordance with those qualities (fr. 68). Teachers should sacrificially and lovingly commit themselves to needy students (fr. 44; 80; col. 3b). If

---

[5]David Konstan et al., eds., *Philodemus: On Frank Criticism*, SBLTT 43 (Atlanta: Scholars Press, 1998), 67.

treatment fails, they should try over and over again (fr. 63-64; 69). If they receive abuse from immature students during the therapeutic process, they should endure it patiently (fr. 70-71). Teachers were to "persistently tame people into love for themselves" when faced with indifference to treatment (fr. 86.2-5).[6] This adaptive and gradual process of treating the weak aimed at their eventual health and growth out of immaturity. Any allowances for the weak to remain immature were temporary, for the teacher loved the weak student and sought his salvation, the person's complete freedom from pain.

Paul on Therapy for the Weak

How does Philodemus's approach compare to Paul's? As I will argue, Paul and Philodemus exhibit both similarities and differences concerning pastoral care for the weak. Paul, like Philodemus, urged believers to adapt to the weak in love out of a concern to protect their vulnerable moral character from harm. However, unlike Philodemus (and against a common interpretation of 1 Cor 8:1–11:1), Paul did not envision this care as a form of psychological therapy by which more mature believers were to lead the immature weak out of their weakness and into self-sufficient maturity. Rather, Paul conceived of building up the weak in a qualitatively different way.

It is necessary first to provide a brief overview of the problem in 1 Corinthians 8:1–11:1 before beginning to interpret Paul's solution in comparative perspective with Philodemus's treatment.

Overview of 1 Corinthians 8:1–11:1. These chapters concern how Corinthian believers should relate to one another with respect to the consumption of food that had been previously offered in pagan sacrifice. Some believers apparently ate this food freely and publicly (1 Cor 8:9-10; 10:25-29), likely citing their knowledge of God as creator and Lord of all, even over idol food, as support (1 Cor 8:4-6). Other believers, however, had similar knowledge of God as Lord, but did not hold that knowledge in the same way when they ate idol food (1 Cor 8:7).

---

[6]Translation from Konstan et al., *Philodemus: On Frank Criticism*, 89.

For these "weak" believers, to eat idol food was necessarily to eat it as a religious act toward pagan gods, because they had a "weak consciousness" habituated toward pagan worship. Their "consciousness" was basically their own self-awareness of their behavior. Their consciousness retrospectively monitored their moral responsibility to God as they acted (see, e.g., Rom 2:15; 9:1; 1 Cor 4:4; 2 Cor 1:12). If they saw others eating idol food and were pressured to do the same, they could not avoid eating the food with the consciousness of doing so as an idolatrous act of worship to pagan gods, even if it was not understood as such by others. By eating, they committed idolatry against God; they were being "destroyed" and being caused "to fall into sin" (1 Cor 8:11, 13). This consumption undermined their Christian commitment to the one God. Additional knowledge about God or idol food could not instantly change their weak consciousness, or else Paul would have attempted to supply it. Instead, Paul urged that others should lovingly build up the weak, not "destroy" them by continuing their current behavior (1 Cor 8:8-13; 10:23–11:1).

Similarities between Philodemus and Paul. How are Paul's guidelines to build up the weak in 1 Corinthians 8:1–11:1 similar to what we found in Philodemus? I note four similarities that are relevant for our purposes here.

First, Paul was concerned with the moral lives of individual believers (including, but not limited to, their knowledge and consciousness). The well-being of each believer's faith was bound up with the shape of this moral life. The weak did not have the same personal resources in knowledge or consciousness as others with respect to eating idol food, and were thus more vulnerable to harm (1 Cor 8:7-13). Paul uses the same vocabulary as Philodemus to describe believers as "weak" in 1 Corinthians 8:1–11:1 (*asthenēs*, see *OFC* fr. 59 above). Other believers did not have the same vulnerability as the weak, but they must beware lest their knowledge and unhindered consciousness desensitize them to idolatrous acts, whether their own acts or those of weak believers (1 Cor 10:14-21).

Second, Paul showed compassion for the weak and did not abandon or segregate them from communal life. The weak were to be treated as siblings "for whom Christ died" (1 Cor 8:11). Paul drew on his own model of adaptive care for the weak in order to lead others to care for them (1 Cor 9:19-23; 10:31–11:1).

Third, Paul assumed that the responsibility of care for the weak fell to other community members in general. The responsibility was not limited to Paul or other leading figures (1 Cor 8:9-13; 10:23–11:1). Fourth, the central means by which Paul sought to build up the weak were (1) love (see 1 Cor 8:1) and (2) adaptation to the weak believer's circumstances. For Paul, adaptation involved abstinence from idol food served in temples (1 Cor 8:10) and from idol food whose cultic origins had been declared at a meal in the presence of the weak (1 Cor 10:23–11:1; see also Paul's model of adaptation in 1 Cor 9:19-23).

These similarities help to ground the validity of the comparison between Paul and Philodemus. However, it is important to consider one further possible similarity. Some scholars would argue that both Paul and Philodemus aimed to bring the weak out of their weakness by adaptive therapy. This view deserves some elaboration. As we will see, whether one shares this view becomes very important for understanding Paul's vision of building up the weak.

In this view, building up the weak in 1 Corinthians 8:1–11:1 was essentially the same process as leading the immature into maturity via frank criticism, as seen in Philodemus. Paul intended for the more mature (those with knowledge) to build up weak believers' knowledge and consciousness by rational, therapeutic persuasion rooted in the gospel. Much like Philodemus was willing to bear with the weaknesses of the less mature and to reform them gradually, Paul championed long-term, adaptive therapy for the weak so that they could gain the knowledge and consciousness that all mature believers should have concerning idol food.

While many would not interpret these chapters with Philodemus specifically in mind, it is common for scholars to arrive at this understanding of building up the weak. In support for this reading, scholars point to the inherent criticism in the label "weak," and to their apparent immaturity due to lacking knowledge (just as the weak were immature and lacked knowledge in Philodemus). If Paul commanded believers to eat idol food bought in a market or served at a host's table without concern for its relationship to consciousness (1 Cor 10:25-27), some argue that this would have gradually helped the weak to grow more comfortable with the food and thus to mature in knowledge and consciousness. Others argue that public abstinence for the weak (as in 10:28-29) would have shamed them into abandoning their immaturity over time.

Is this what Paul meant by building up the weak, namely, persuading the weak to grow out of their weakness? At first glance, one might answer affirmatively. I argue, however, that Paul and Philodemus are significantly different at this point, especially when one considers other differences that emerge between them.

Differences between Philodemus and Paul. Among other differences that might be discussed, the following are particularly important for our focus on what Paul meant by building up the weak.

First, Paul rendered differences in personal knowledge and consciousness of idol food irrelevant for one's standing before God. Philodemus, in contrast, would have assumed that these differences followed from moral maturity or immaturity, given that they were rooted in knowledge. Paul partially affirmed the theological position of the knowers that idols and idol food are nothing (1 Cor 8:4-6; see also 1 Cor 10:19, 25-26). However, in 1 Corinthians 8:8, Paul deemed the consumption of idol food irrelevant for one's relationship to God: "Food does not bring us near to God; we are no worse if we do not eat, and no better if we do." In other words, for Paul there was no inherent theological difference between consumption of idol food and abstinence from it. It was true that some circumstances could make consumption of idol food a sinful act (eating with a weak consciousness; eating when it would cause the weak to sin; eating as part of an act of worship to a pagan god [see 1 Cor 10:14-22]). Yet the act of eating the food in itself was neither sinful nor beneficial for the believer. For a believer's standing before God, there was no inherently important difference between possessing or lacking the knowledge and consciousness that enabled consumption of idol food.

In other cases, Paul readily encouraged growth in knowledge as part of development as a believer (for example, 1 Cor 12:8; 14:19, 31). Moreover, Paul was no stranger to using caustic criticism to lead others to maturity, even if he arguably had a different conception of this process than Philodemus (also note his use of the same word for frank speech, *parrēsia*, in 2 Cor 3:12; 7:4; Phil 1:20; Philem 8). In 1 Corinthians 8:1–11:1, however, an increase in knowledge of God or knowledge of idol food for the weak does not seem to be the goal.

The second difference is that the believers who build up the weak are not thereby more mature in faith than the weak. In contrast, Philodemus would assume that those who treat the weak are more mature morally (otherwise, they have no claim to do so). Paul accuses those who have knowledge of sinning "against Christ" in their destructive behavior toward the weak (1 Cor 8:12). Their lack of love for the weak displayed their lack of real knowledge and thus their immaturity (see 1 Cor 8:2-3). The weak were limited in knowledge and consciousness in comparison with others, but Paul did not clearly link this limitation to immaturity in faith. Instead he minimized the relevance of this limitation for faith in God (1 Cor 8:8). Eating or avoiding idol food was irrelevant for maturity as a believer.

Third, therefore, Paul's goal in this instance was not that all believers would achieve one, "mature" state of personal knowledge and consciousness of idol food. Philodemus, in contrast, envisions salvation as the attainment of a particular state of moral character with its knowledge, emotions, reason, and so on. He could not have claimed, like Paul, that a difference in knowledge involving moral vulnerability was irrelevant to moral maturity. For Paul, however, building up the weak did not mean curing them with therapy based on one version of knowledge and consciousness of idol food.

These differences between Paul and Philodemus make a critical contribution to our understanding of what Paul meant by building up the weak. By acknowledging these differences, we are steered away from the interpretation that building up the weak involves curing them of their immaturity, as in Philodemus's philosophical therapy. For Paul, it cannot be true that building up the weak meant curing them of their weakness, because he did not consider the weakness inherently relevant for mature faith in God. Paul had a different understanding in this case, one that did not involve increasing the knowledge of the weak or healing their consciousness with gentle critique-therapy over time. This negative result pushes us closer to what Paul did mean.

The similarities identified above remain valid. Paul remains concerned about the weak believers' health and salvation. He approaches them lovingly and adaptively like Philodemus would. Yet he has a different conception of what "health," "maturity," and "salvation" entail, and a different conception of the role others play in this salvation. *Comparatively, Paul puts less value in the achievement of specific psychological states and human knowledge, and more value in a believer's allegiance to God whatever their psychological circumstances. Building up the weak has more to do with supporting their faithfulness to God in their weakness rather than transcending their psychological limitations.* While space prohibits the treatment this topic deserves, the following sketch promotes further reflection upon what Paul meant by building up the weak.

Paul's Vision for Building Up the Weak

The problem facing the weak was that they succumbed to pressure and ate idol food as an idolatrous act. Paul did not attempt to make the weak self-sufficient by augmenting their knowledge and consciousness so that they might eat freely or resist the pressure, but attempted to eliminate or mitigate the external circumstances causing harm. Especially problematic was the pressure caused by other believers who consumed idol food in the presence of the weak. Thus, building up the weak referred, first of all, to protecting the weak person's faith in God by removing harmful circumstances. Believers were to abstain from the food that caused trouble for the weak, thereby offering them support within loving, sacrificial relationships based on the gospel (treating them as siblings, as those for whom Christ died, 8:11). Put simply, building up the weak meant not leading them to commit idolatry.

Yet beyond this, Paul envisioned this new support to contribute to the weak believers' faith in God. At the conclusion of this passage, Paul states the ultimate reason for adapting to the weak: "For I am not seeking my own good but the good of many, so that they may be saved" (1 Cor 10:33; see also 1 Cor 9:19-22). It was not Paul, but Christ who was the ultimate model to imitate in caring for the weak unto their salvation (1 Cor 11:1). By linking believers' adaptation to the weak to their ultimate salvation by God, Paul claimed that God himself was at work for salvation of the weak through their relationships with other believers.

The weak believers' experience of God's salvation through the help of others was part of what the gospel meant for them as weak believers. Through the help of others they were being preserved as blameless in anticipation of the coming the day of the Lord (1 Cor 1:8). Without this help from others, they would stand separated from God's saving purposes for them through the body of Christ (see also 1 Cor 12:7, 12-27). Paul was not for a separate assembly of the weak! The weak would receive support from others as God's necessary intervention to save them from idolatry. They would exercise their faith in God against idolatry through greater dependence on other believers. The weak's salvation would not come from achieving a cognitive and psychological state of individual self-sufficiency. Rather, salvation arose from trusting God through dependence on others in their self-*in*sufficiency.

The weak's faith developed in that it operated in a renewed mode of dependence on others, and thus upon God. Embracing this dependence would evidence their maturity in faith, not their immaturity.

This dependence strengthened their commitment to God against idolatry, and properly ordered their faith to God's saving work for them through other believers in Corinth.

In this chapter, we have analyzed similarity and difference side by side, allowing Paul and Philodemus to speak in their own voices to similar questions and problems. Paul and Philodemus concerned themselves with care for the weak through love and adaptation to their circumstances. Paul was aware, like Philodemus, of the critical importance of believers' individual moral lives and of the issues raised when members differed in their moral character. However, our comparison has shown that Paul, unlike Philodemus, did not envision the weak to be cured by the development of their knowledge and consciousness of idol food. Instead, other believers should build up the weak believers' faith in God by offering them relational support to mitigate harmful situations, by strengthening their faith in God against idolatry, and by directing them to faith in God's saving work for them through other believers.

AN OVERVIEW OF DIFFERENCES BETWEEN PHILODEMUS AND PAUL

Table 2.1. Overview

For Philodemus	For Paul
The weak were cognitively and psychologically immature in comparison to their caregivers.	Unlike the other believers whose role was to build them up, the weak were relatively limited in knowledge and consciousness, but were not thereby less mature in faith.
The weak were treated by adaptive frank criticism based on Epicurean philosophy to achieve one, complete model of human knowledge and psychology.	The weak were built up by receiving support from others in order to be faithful to God in their weakness, not by achieving a particular state of knowledge and consciousness through therapy.
The weak became more self-sufficient and less dependent on others as they matured through therapy.	The weak's embrace of dependence upon others, and thus dependence upon God, evidenced mature faith.

For Further Reading

Primary Sources

Babbit, Frank Cole, trans. *Plutarch: Moralia*. Vol. 1. LCL 197. Cambridge, MA: Harvard University Press, 1927.

Bailey, Cyril, ed. *Epicurus: The Extant Remains with Short Critical Apparatus, Translation and Notes*. Oxford: Oxford University Press, 1926.

Basore, John W., trans. *Seneca: Moral Essays*. Vol. 2. LCL 254. Cambridge, MA: Harvard University Press, 1932.

Grummere, Richard M., trans. *Seneca: Epistles*. 3 Vols. LCL 75-77. Cambridge, MA: Harvard University Press, 1917–1925.

Indelli, Giovanni, and Voula Tsouna-McKirahan, eds. *Philodemus: On Choices and Avoidances*. La Scuola di Epicuro 15. Naples: Bibliopolis, 1995.

Konstan, David, et al., eds. *Philodemus: On Frank Criticism*. SBLTT 43. Atlanta: Scholars Press, 1998.

Secondary Sources

Barclay, John M. G. "Faith and Self-Detachment from Cultural Norms: A Study in Romans 14–15." *ZNW* 104 (2013): 192-208.

Eastman, Susan Grove. *Paul and the Person: Reframing Paul's Anthropology*. Grand Rapids: Eerdmans, 2017.

Glad, Clarence E. *Paul and Philodemus: Adaptability in Epicurean and Early Christian Psychagogy*. NovTSup 81. Leiden; New York: Brill, 1995.

Malherbe, Abraham J. "Hellenistic Moralists and the New Testament." In *Aufstieg und Niedergang der Römischen Welt*, II.26.1, edited by Wolfgang Haase and Hildegard Temporini, 267-333. Berlin: de Gruyter, 1992.

Nussbaum, Martha C. *The Therapy of Desire*. Princeton, NJ: Princeton University Press, 1994.

Sampley, J. Paul. "Paul and Frankness." In *Paul in the Greco-Roman World: A Handbook*, edited by J. Paul Sampley, vol. 1, 2nd ed., 303-30. New York: Bloomsbury T&T Clark, 2016.

Stowers, Stanley. "Paul on the Use and Abuse of Reason." In *Greeks, Romans, and Christians*, edited by David L. Balch, Everett Ferguson, and Wayne A. Meeks, 253-86. Minneapolis: Fortress, 1990.

Tsouna, Voula. *The Ethics of Philodemus*. Oxford: Oxford University Press, 2007.

DISCUSSION QUESTIONS

1. In 1 Corinthians 8:1–11:1, why does Paul seem to avoid a correction of the weak, whereas he wholeheartedly corrects others elsewhere in the letter, as in 1 Corinthians 3, 5, and 6?

2. Does Paul operate with Philodemus's model of therapy for the weak in Romans 14:1–15:6 or Galatians 6:1-5? Why or why not?

3. Beyond the issue of treating the weak particularly, what are the most significant theological and anthropological similarities and differences between Paul and an Epicurean like Philodemus with respect to moral growth?

4. How might Paul's vision for building up the weak in 1 Corinthians 8:1–11:1 be theologically appropriated by Christians today?

3

WHY CAN'T WE BE FRIENDS?

PAUL AND ARISTOTLE ON FRIENDSHIP

DAVID E. BRIONES

EVERYONE IS FAMILIAR WITH FRIENDSHIP. We make friends. We lose friends. We have friends. We are friends. It is an essential part of our humanity. But do we ever stop and think about friendship? What *is* friendship? What makes for a good or bad friendship? How is a friendship formed and sustained? What is the ultimate goal of friendship?

Ancient philosophers often reflected on these sorts of questions, especially Aristotle. He devotes two major sections to the topic of friendship in his philosophical treatise *Nicomachean Ethics*. His work provocatively challenges the way people understand friendship, how they practice it, and the ultimate goal of friendship. Aristotle's thoughts are so influential that all later thinkers, everyone from pagan philosophers like Seneca to Christian theologians like Thomas Aquinas, draw from him to varying degrees.

Another person who had influential thoughts on friendship was the apostle Paul. In fact, it has become commonplace to compare his letter to the Philippians with the work of ancient philosophers on the topic of friendship. But as you can guess, Paul and Aristotle describe friendship from two distinct vantage points. One is a Christian missionary and theologian; the other, a Greek philosopher and scientist. Of course, there are similarities between the two at some levels, but at the deeper level of comparison, major differences emerge. The most striking is the presence of God in human friendship.

The question of God's presence or absence is not a moot point. It drastically changes the way a person understands the nature, practice, and goal of friendship. To see this, we will first describe Aristotle's *philosophy* of friendship before turning to Paul's *theology* of friendship, ultimately leading to a final section explaining why the two can't be friends.

ARISTOTLE'S PHILOSOPHY OF FRIENDSHIP

Let's begin by asking, How did Aristotle define friendship in *Nicomachean Ethics*? His clearest definition appears in 8.2.3-5. He insists that, to be friends, two traits must be present. The first is the giving and receiving of friendly affection that, over time, grows into "love" for the other's own sake. The second is a mutual concern to seek the good of the other person with the other person's awareness. Imagine a friendly interaction between Socrates and Plato. They are friends, which means their friendly affection is slowly growing into love. But this friendship is not one-way. Socrates seeks Plato's good, and Plato desires Socrates's good. It is a give-and-take relationship. If Socrates only gives and Plato only takes (and I think we're familiar with this kind of relationship), then they don't share a friendship. Friendship requires a back and forth of affectionate concern.

But a crucial component in all of this is shared awareness. Socrates and Plato must be aware of their mutual affection and goodwill toward one another. It's kind of like that awkward stage in any relationship where you have the infamous DTR talk—Defining The Relationship. It's uncomfortable and awkward, but it's necessary. Whether you're searching for a spouse or looking for a friend, a shared awareness must exist. If it does, Plato has a friend in Socrates. If not, he has a mere acquaintance.

Virtue friendship. Once Aristotle outlines these two traits in every friendship, he argues that there are three forms of friendship: those "[1] based on virtue, [2] on utility, and [3] on pleasure" (*Eth. eud.* 7.2.13; cf. *Nic. Eth.* 8.3). Those based on *utility* and *pleasure* are considered friendships in only a qualified sense. The friend is not loved for being who he "is" (*Nic. Eth.* 8.3.2) but for what he provides. A friendship based on utility will dissolve when, for example, Socrates can no longer get Plato a discount on his toga. A friendship based on pleasure will end when Plato no longer wishes to join Socrates in philosophical discourse. But a friendship based on virtue is entirely different. A virtue-friend will desire the good of his friends "for their own sake," and they will love each other "for themselves." So, say Socrates and Plato enjoy a virtuous friendship. Plato would love Socrates, and Socrates would love Plato, not for what they do (pleasure) or provide (utility), but for who they *are* (virtue). And who they are *essentially*, Aristotle argues, is virtuous. Their virtue, not financial advantage or pleasurable moments, leads them to love one another.

One qualification needs to be made here. Just because Aristotle distinguishes between friendships based on utility, pleasure, and virtue, that does not mean utility and pleasure play no role in virtue friendships. Remember, friendship is reciprocal, consisting of giving *and* receiving. Sometimes, Plato will be on the giving end; at other times, he'll be on the receiving end. But if he's friends with Socrates, they will be "beneficial to one another" (8.3.6). They will benefit one another, but not in the utilitarian sense. Virtue friendships promote a unique kind of mutual benefit, and what makes it unique is its *basis*.

The basis of virtue friendship, strangely enough, is self-love. You may be thinking, "How can friends mutually benefit one another if they only love themselves?" Aristotle is not promoting a *selfish* self-love, but a *virtuous* self-love. Aristotle explains: when we love and care for a friend, those feelings of concern are "derived from the feelings of regard which we entertain *for ourselves*" (9.4.1; my italics). Again, Socrates, as a virtuous friend, will desire good for his friend Plato because he desires good for himself, and Plato will do likewise. So, it makes sense for Aristotle to conclude, "Therefore, the good man ought to be a lover of self, since he will then *both* benefit himself by acting nobly *and* aid his fellows" (9.8.7; my italics). The both-and statement above shows that self-love is virtuous because it benefits both parties. It isn't self-serving. In loving himself, Socrates is also loving Plato. No wonder Aristotle calls a friend "another self" (9.4.5) who shares "one soul" with you and with whom you hold all things in common (9.8.2; cf. 8.12.1). In the closeness of friendship, souls intermingle. In modern lingo, friends are kindred spirits who complete one another.

Now one underlying assumption regarding this self-love is worth mentioning: virtue is a *prerequisite* for true friendship. The perfect form of friendship, writes Aristotle, is between "those who resemble each other in virtue" (8.3.6). This requires two parties to embody virtuous qualities of the mind and life (both intellectual and moral virtue) *prior* to initiating a friendship. Socrates or Plato would be obvious candidates for this kind of friendship. But what about Emperor Nero or Judas Iscariot? Not so much. No virtue, no friendship.

The role of God in friendship. But what about God? Does he play any role in Aristotle's philosophy of friendship? The short answer is "no." Aristotle's god plays no direct role in human friendship. God is entirely self-sufficient. He has no need for friendship. Only humans do. They need friends. That's how humans achieve self-knowledge or receive a benefit—through "another self." Humans, in other words, require means. God, however, has no need of such means. He is "a seamless, simple whole, so perfect and so self-contained," that he is rendered "incapable of friendship."[1] Friendship, then, is impossible between the transcendent god and needy humans. Aristotle did not believe in a personal god who relates to humanity, or in a god who hears the prayers of people. According to the philosopher, god is not concerned with humanity's well-being. Relating to people would only limit his perfection. Since a self-contemplating god needs no friends, the only role this transcendent, impersonal god can play in human friendship is as a model for unequal relationships. God solely functions as a removed pattern for imitation (cf. 8.12.5; 8.14.4; 9.1.7; *Eth. eud.* 7.3.2-3). Human friendship is exclusively human.

---

[1] Lorraine S. Pangle, *Aristotle and the Philosophy of Friendship* (Cambridge: Cambridge University Press, 2003), 154.

To summarize Aristotle's philosophical perspective, a friendship between Socrates and Plato can only exist if there is a reciprocity of affectionate concern to seek one another's good with a shared awareness. The best form of friendship is the one based on virtue, which is obviously not devoid of utility or pleasure. Virtuous self-love makes friendship mutually beneficial. It is the basis of virtue friendships. But in order to enter into a friendship of virtue, each person must first be virtuous. It is a necessary prerequisite. Aristotle's god may be perfect, but he plays no part in this perfect form of friendship. His god is perfectly self-sufficient, transcendent, and impersonal.

Paul could never have entered into a virtue friendship as Aristotle articulates it. Paul couldn't conceive of a friendship without God's presence. But that's not to say there aren't many similarities between Paul and Aristotle, as we will soon find out.

Paul's Theology of Friendship

A comparison between Paul and Aristotle on friendship may seem futile, at first glance. Paul doesn't use the words "friend" or "friendship" in his writings. He only describes friendship conceptually. But even then, he lacks the philosophical precision of Aristotle. It therefore doesn't seem as if a comparison would be fruitful, let alone possible. However, when we consider the many verbal, conceptual, and thematic parallels that New Testament scholars have discovered between Philippians and *Nicomachean Ethics* 8–9, a comparison is certainly possible, even fruitful. Especially noteworthy is Paul's use of the terms *koinōnia* (fellowship/partnership/friendship; Phil 1:5, 7; 3:10; 4:14, 15), and *phronēsis* (like-mindedness/understanding/care; Phil 1:7; 2:2, 5; 3:15, 19; 4:2, 10). These key words, which were standard elements of friendship language in the ancient world, help bridge the comparative gap between Paul and Aristotle.

The ideal definition of friendship. Unlike Aristotle, Paul does not present us with an explicit definition of friendship or with a categorization and explanation of the diverse forms of friendship. Instead, Paul provides an ideal (though implicit) definition of his friendship with the Philippians by employing the key words mentioned above, *koinōnia* and *phronēsis*. We find that Paul and the Philippians enjoy a fellowship of gift and suffering, with God as the divine source in a triangular friendship. This is what friendship in Christ looks like.

Two traits appear in Paul's theology of friendship. The first is a reciprocity of gifts (immaterial and material) between Paul and the Philippians, which stems from a mutual *phronēsis*—a way of thinking, feeling, and acting patterned after Jesus Christ (Phil 2:5-11). Two verses plainly convey this. In Philippians 1:7, Paul says that it is right for him "to feel" (*phronein*) confidently about the Philippians. Then, in Philippians 4:10, the Philippians express their "concern" (*phronein*) for Paul through their gift. The same word is used in these two verses because the same sentiment drives Paul's and the Philippians' regard for one another. A shared *phronēsis* binds them together in a loving, reciprocal friendship.

But what exactly do they reciprocate? To begin with, Paul and the Philippians reciprocate *affectionate concern* for one another. Every time Paul recalls their fellowship, he thanks God and prays for the Philippians "with joy" (Phil 1:3-5). He says, "I hold you in my heart" and "yearn for you all with the affection of Christ Jesus" (Phil 1:7-8 ESV). And he desires to be with them for their good (1:25-27; 2:24). Imprisoned, he sends Timothy to learn of their progress in the faith in order that Paul's heart may be encouraged (Phil 2:19). The fact that Paul sends Timothy to the community demonstrates his affectionate concern; only a "like-minded person" genuinely concerned for the community is fit to visit his beloved congregation (Phil 2:20). Paul dispels the anxiety of the Philippians with comforting exhortations to pray and to receive the peace of God (Phil 4:6-7). In every situation they remain his beloved, whom he loves and longs for: his joy, crown, and boast (Phil 2:12-16; 4:1). In return, the Philippians express affectionate concern for Paul. They sent Epaphroditus to care for him spiritually and financially (Phil 2:25-30; 4:18). Notably, this sprang from a revived *phronēsis*, a Christ-like way of thinking, feeling, and acting that couldn't be expressed earlier, according to Philippians 4:10.

Moreover, Paul and the Philippians reciprocate *sacrificial service* for one another's joy. Paul likens his ministry to a sacrificial drink offering and service for their faith (Phil 2:17), which is directly connected to their joy (Phil 2:17-18; cf. 1:25). In response, so also their material gift for Paul is considered a sacrifice (Phil 4:18; 2:17) and service (Phil 2:17, 30). The outcome of this exchange is mutual joy (Phil 2:17-18).

Finally, Paul and the Philippians reciprocate *prayer* to God on behalf of one another for present and ultimate salvation. Paul prays that their love would abound to "approve what is excellent" and to become "pure and blameless for the day of Christ" (Phil 1:9-11 ESV). He beckons them to "work out [their] salvation with fear and trembling" (Phil 2:12), and so become "pure and blameless" in the midst of a world gone awry (Phil 2:14-15). In the same way, just as Paul prays for their final salvation (Phil 1:4, 9-11; cf. 1:28; 2:12), so the Philippians will also pray for Paul's salvation, physically from prison and eschatologically from death (Phil 1:19). By praying to God, Paul positions God as the divine source on which Paul and the Philippians mutually depend for their salvation (cf. Phil 1:6; 2:12-13).

The second relational dynamic in Paul's ideal definition of friendship is enduring suffering on behalf of the other. In Christ, Paul and the Philippians have access to a particular mindset best exemplified by Christ's humiliation on behalf of others (Phil 2:5-11). Paul exemplifies this christological mindset by suffering on behalf of the Philippians. In Philippians 1:12-18, he makes known the advancement of the gospel through his suffering (Phil 1:12). Although Paul considers death gain (Phil 1:21), he nevertheless stifles the desire for gain because remaining in the flesh will mean "fruitful labor" (Phil 1:22), primarily for the Philippians. It is "more necessary for [their] sake" (Phil 1:24). In the background of all of this is God in Christ by the Spirit. He is the one behind the progress of the gospel in Philippians 1:12 and of their faith in Philippians 1:25. Paul willingly suffers for the Philippians' benefit, but it is God who actively works in and through Paul on behalf of the Philippian church.

Similarly, to benefit Paul, the Philippians send a material gift, likened to a sacrifice (Phil 4:18; 2:17) and service (Phil 2:17, 30). By doing so, they share in his suffering (Phil 4:14). They are fellow-partakers of his chains (Phil 1:7). They are engaged in the same conflict as the apostle (Phil 1:29-30). Their struggle has two components: (1) theologically, they suffer as those united to Christ, and (2) socially, they suffer shame as those associated with a prisoner whom the law deemed a social deviant. But the most interesting fact about the Philippians' participation with Paul in gift and suffering is that God is behind it all. He revived the Philippians' concern to send their gift to Paul (Phil 4:10) and so share in his suffering (Phil 4:14).

Like Aristotle, it seems that Paul also defines friendship as a reciprocity of goodwill and a mutual concern to seek the good of the other person for their sake, with a shared awareness. He just uses different language to talk about it. But one insurmountable difference is obvious: there is a third party in Paul's theological definition of friendship. The triune God—Father, Son, and Spirit—appears on the scene as the vertical party whose presence naturally reconfigures the horizontal dimensions of friendship. But how precisely does he do so? How, for instance, does God reconfigure the essential components of friendship mentioned above: self-love and virtue?

The role of self-love in Pauline friendship. Does the concept of self-love appear in Paul's writings? Philippians 2:3 suggests that the answer is "no": "Do nothing from selfish ambition or conceit, but in humility count others more significant than yourselves" (ESV). Counting others more significant than yourself suggests that you don't consider yourself at all. Yet, as I frequently say in my Hermeneutics course, "we simply need to keep reading." Philippians 2:4 says, "Let each of you look *not only* to his own interests, *but also* to the interests of others" (ESV, my italics). This verse prevents Christians from swinging the pendulum to one extreme (radical altruism: caring exclusively for others) or another (radical egoism: caring exclusively for oneself). Like Aristotle, Paul lands somewhere in between.

By not eliminating self-love in Christian friendship, Paul finds a happy medium that ensures reciprocity in the church. He promotes a virtuous self-love, one that includes the interests of others *primarily* and one's own interests *secondarily*. Aristotle would certainly rejoice at this thought, especially since Paul describes friendship (*koinōnia*) as being of "one soul" (Phil 2:2), "one mind" (Phil 2:2), and "one spirit" (Phil 1:27), as those who strive together with "one soul" (Phil 1:27) and share the "same love" (Phil 2:2). How can this be any different from Aristotle's view that a friend is "another self," a second self, with whom compassion, affection, and sympathy are shared? All this might have led Aristotle to reason: "Well, if Paul affirms that a friend is another self, and he promotes self-love as mutually beneficial, then he must see self-love as the *basis* of reciprocity." But his reasoning would overlook one fundamental reality in Christ: God's active presence in friendship.

Paul's inclusion of God within Christian friendship radically re-shapes (and makes possible) Aristotle's concept of self-love. The *basis* of reciprocity is not self-love, as it is in Aristotle. The *basis* of friendship is the presence of a divine party, who energizes one's willingness and activity, who provides what is needed to give to the other, and who ensures that a return will be made. The triune God—Father, Son, and Spirit—is the *basis* of friendships in Christ.

This configuration can be seen in the way Paul strategically incorporates God in the common interests of friends. In Philippians 2:20-21, Paul not only speaks of one's own interests and the interests of others, but also mentions the interests of Jesus Christ. By introducing the interests of a divine actor onto the scene of Christian friendship, Paul redefines what is meant by self- and other-oriented interest. As John Barclay explains, "One serves the other's interests not for their sake in isolation, but for their sake *in their relation to God*. Similarly, however one views one's own interests will be determined by one's standing *in relation to Christ*."[2] The interests of God in Christ by the Spirit—the Lord over both parties (Phil 1:2; cf. 2:11, 19; 3:8, 20)—determine the self- and other-oriented interests of human friendship. United to God and one another in Christ, Christian friendship now finds it basis in the triune God.

---

[2]John M. G. Barclay, "Benefiting Others and Benefit to Oneself: Seneca and Paul on 'Altruism,'" in *Paul and Seneca in Dialogue*, ed. Joseph R. Dodson and David E. Briones, Ancient Philosophy & Religion 2 (Leiden: Brill, 2017), 122.

Paul also presents God in Christ as the basis of reciprocity in the three-way relational pattern in Philippians 4:10-20. Verse 10 not only incorporates God into Paul and the Philippians' relationship but also presents him as the ultimate giver *to* Paul *through* the Philippians. As noted earlier, *God* revived the Philippians' concern and generosity toward Paul in prison, so Paul rightly returns gratitude to the Giver (Phil 4:10). That God is the one on whom Paul ultimately depends for material abundance is clear from Philippians 4:11-13. Paul replaces "self-sufficiency" with "Christ-sufficiency." He depends on the one who empowers him (Phil 4:13) to experience the state of material abundance (Phil 4:12). And yet, according to verse 18, God uses the Philippians to accomplish that end. They are mediators of his abundance.

The reverse is also true. Paul and the Philippians enjoy a fellowship in giving *and* receiving (Phil 4:15). "My God," Paul exclaims, "will supply every need of yours according to his riches in glory in Christ Jesus" (Phil 4:19 ESV). Understanding "need" as material lack, since that is how it is used in Philippians 4:16, and interpreting "riches" as both material and heavenly riches, since it comes from God in heaven but appears tangibly on earth, enables one to see the three-way relational pattern: God's supply will stream *through* Paul *to* the Philippians. Thus, Philippians 4:10-18 expresses Paul's dependence on God *through* the Philippians, while 4:19-20 envisions a time when the Philippians will depend on God *through* Paul, exhibiting a characteristic pattern of friendship in Christ, shown in figure 1.

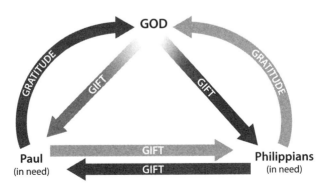

Figure 1. Three-way pattern of friendship in Christ

The *basis* of reciprocity illustrated in figure 1 is a common Lord whose divine supply is mediated in and through friends in Christ to meet one another's needs. From Paul's theological perspective, God is not only at the center but also at the beginning and end of every Christian friendship.

The role of virtue in Pauline friendship. But what about the role of virtue in friendship? Is it the same as Aristotle's construal? As we saw in his *Nicomachean Ethics*, virtue is a prerequisite for true friendships to exist. Is this the case in the book of Philippians? The word *virtue* only appears in Philippians 4:8, but the absence of the term should not lead us to conclude that the concept is absent. One must appeal to the broader context. Especially relevant to the question is Philippians 1:27-30. In this text, we find that friendship and virtue are created through faith in the gospel of Christ, making virtue a *result* rather than a *prerequisite* of Christian friendship.

In Philippians 1:27-30, Paul begins by exhorting the Philippians to do one thing: "Only let your manner of life be worthy of the gospel of Christ" (Phil 1:27 ESV).[3] In the ancient world, to be called "worthy" was essentially equivalent to being called "virtuous." But the way Paul describes a life that is worthy goes against ancient conceptions of worth and virtue. According to Philippians 1:27-28, friends who are "worthy" will, with "one spirit" and "one mind," stand and strive for the "faith of the gospel." Christian friendship therefore consists of standing united in suffering and gospel advancement, despite persecution. This is what Paul means by living a "worthy" (or, we could say, "virtuous") life. But that's not a prerequisite for Christian friendship. Living worthily or becoming virtuous is a *result* of God's work in and through the gospel of Christ.

Look back at 1:27-28. Behind the human worth and virtuous actions listed is a divine source, which appears in the critical phrase "and that from God" (Phil 1:28). God is the source of their "salvation" (Phil 1:28), but he is also the source of their "worthy" lifestyle described in

---

[3]For an expansion of the ideas in this section, please see David E. Briones, *Paul's Financial Policy: A Socio-Theological Approach* (LNTS 494; London: Bloomsbury, 2013), 93-95.

Philippians 1:27-28. Paul points to God as the Christian's source of worth and virtue. To support this claim, Paul, in Philippians 1:28-29, depicts God as the giver of faith, suffering (and the perseverance to endure it), and salvation. Those three gifts cover the beginning, middle, and end of the Christian life. And all of it, from start to finish, is energized by the power of God's grace (Phil 1:6, 29; 2:12-13).

For Aristotle, *doing* precedes *being*. One who does virtuous things is a person worthy of friendship. But, for Paul, *being* precedes *doing*. Only one who has become a friend of God by virtue of union with his Son is enabled to act virtuously. Doing virtuous acts *confirms* one's being considered worthy by God. The source of the church's worth resides in the gospel of Christ (Phil 1:27), where worth is divinely created rather than naturally cultivated. Once the gospel takes hold of people (cf. Phil 3:12), they become what they are, as it calls "worth" and "virtue" into being. This is the unnerving logic of grace, a radical rationale that challenges and even subverts cultural and philosophical notions of virtue. For Paul, a virtuous friendship is the organic *result* of being incorporated into Christ by faith in the gospel.

PAUL AND ARISTOTLE: THE PARTING OF WAYS

The primary difference between Aristotle and Paul concerns the number of parties involved in friendship. Aristotle promotes a linear conception of friendship, with two parties in reciprocal exchange. But Paul endorses a circular conception of friendship, envisioning God as the necessary party who works in and through friends in Christ. In infinite circularity, all things flow from him, through him, and to him (Rom 11:36), and those in Christ are caught up in a divine momentum of gift and gratitude in friendship with God and others. Contrary to Aristotle, God plays a direct role in Christian friendships. He is not simply a removed model for imitation. To be sure, Paul affirms a Creator-creature distinction and divine transcendence (Rom 11:33-36), but friendship between God, Paul, and the Philippians still exists. Christians can be called "a friend of God" (Jas 2:23 ESV). He provides the particular mindset (understanding/*phronēsis*) in Christ that Christians need for virtuous friendships to thrive (Phil 2:2, 5; 3:15; 4:2, 10), and he is the source of all human virtue (Phil 1:27-30). Paul reties Christian friendship into a three-way bond, with the triune God at the center.

What then becomes of our comparison between Paul and Aristotle? We discover that a conspicuous rift emerges between Paul's theology of friendship and Aristotle's philosophy of friendship—a rift too deep for surface-level similarities to repair. Studying Paul alongside of Aristotle helps us realize how significantly different our Christian friendships are compared to those in the world. At best, their bonds are based on self-produced virtue; at worst, mere usefulness or pleasure. But those who follow Jesus have virtuous friendships, not based on our worth but Christ's worth, not based on reason but revelation, and not based on human activity but God's activity in the church. He freely works in and through his people, and his people voluntarily depend on him for friendships to flourish. God voluntarily entered into the most intimate bond of friendship with believers. It is only fitting, then, that God receives all the glory.

SIMILARITIES AND DIFFERENCES

Table 3.1. Similarities and differences

Aristotle, *Nicomachean Ethics* 8-9	Paul, *The Letter to the Philippians*
God plays no direct role in human friendships.	God plays an essential role in Christian friendships. He gives, energizes, and sustains every act of human generosity. He hears the prayers of his people, and he responds to their needs.
Friends reciprocate goodwill and a mutual concern to seek the good of the other person for their sake, with a shared awareness.	Friends reciprocate affectionate concern for one another, sacrificial service for one another's joy, and prayer to God for one another's ultimate salvation. They also suffer on behalf of one another.
A friend is another self.	A friend is another self.
A virtuous self-love is promoted as the basis of reciprocity or giving and receiving in friendship.	A virtuous self-love is promoted but not as the basis of reciprocity or giving and receiving in friendship. God in Christ by the Spirit is the basis of reciprocity.
Virtue is an essential part of the best form of friendship. In fact, virtue is a prerequisite to choosing a friend.	Virtue is an essential part of friendship in Christ, but it is not a prerequisite for friendship. It is a result of being befriended by God through the gospel.

FOR FURTHER READING

Primary Sources

Aristotle. *Nicomachean Ethics*. Translated by H. Rackham. LCL. London: Harvard University Press, 1982.

Secondary Sources

Barclay, John M. G. "Benefiting Others and Benefit to Oneself: Seneca and Paul on 'Altruism.'" In *Paul and Seneca in Dialogue*, edited by Joseph R. Dodson and David E. Briones, 109-26, Ancient Philosophy & Religion 2. Leiden: Brill, 2017.

Briones, David E. *Paul's Financial Policy: A Socio-Theological Approach*. LNTS 494. London: Bloomsbury, 2013.

Fee, Gordon. *Paul's Letter to the Philippians*. NICNT. Grand Rapids: Eerdmans, 1995.

Fitzgerald, John T. "Paul and Friendship." In *Paul in the Greco-Roman World: A Handbook*, edited by J. Paul Sampley, 319-43. Harrisburg, PA: Trinity Press International, 2003.

Fowl, Stephen. *Philippians*. THNTC. Grand Rapids: Eerdmans, 2005.

Pakaluk, Michael, trans. *Nicomachean Ethics: Books VIII and IX*. Oxford: Oxford University Press, 1998.

Pangle, Lorraine S. *Aristotle and the Philosophy of Friendship*. Cambridge: Cambridge University Press, 2003.

White, L. Michael. "Morality Between Two Worlds: A Paradigm of Friendship in Philippians." In *Greeks, Romans, and Christians: Essays in Honor of Abraham J. Malherbe*, edited by David Balch, Everett Ferguson, and Wayne Meeks, 201-15. Minneapolis: Augsburg Fortress, 1990.

DISCUSSION QUESTIONS

1. In what ways do Aristotle and Paul help you understand the nature, process, and goal of friendship?

2. How do Paul and Aristotle promote self-interest without making it self-serving?

3. What role does virtue play in Aristotle and Paul's definitions of friendship?

4. Do Aristotle and Paul believe in the same God? Why or why not?

4

SLAVES TO THE CULTURE?

ATTITUDES ON SLAVERY IN PAUL AND SENECA

TIMOTHY A. BROOKINS

UNDER THE ROMAN EMPIRE, about one in every four people in Italy was a slave. In those days, slavery was not rooted in racial prejudice. Many people entered slavery as captives of war. Others became slaves through piracy, trade, or self-sale. Ultimately, most of the slave population was comprised of those born into slavery.

As a slave, one was counted as personal property over whom masters wielded absolute legal and physical mastery. Yet quality of life for slaves could vary greatly. For many people, slavery meant a meager diet, grueling labor, and cruel physical abuse, including sexual exploitation. Criminals were consigned to the bitterest forms of slavery, working in the mines or rowing the war ships. On the brighter side, slaves possessed the right to receive wages and to hold property, some received a decent education, and a great many anticipated the likelihood of gaining their freedom by the age of thirty. For the most fortunate, slavery offered a life of provision, relative comfort, and in some cases, upward social and economic mobility. Attitudes about slavery varied, but abolition was virtually never proposed as a moral necessity, much less as a serious socio-structural possibility.

It is a source of consternation for many readers of Paul that his letters never condemn slavery as an institution, although his letters address master-slave relationships on several occasions. The present chapter will focus on Paul's discussion of slavery found in his letter to

Philemon and will set it beside the forty-seventh epistle of the Stoic philosopher Seneca. This juxtaposition makes for an interesting comparison for several reasons. First, Paul and Seneca were almost exact contemporaries and so represent two ways of viewing slavery within the same general cultural context. Second, Paul's letter to Philemon and Seneca's forty-seventh epistle were written at almost exactly the same time (both written ca. AD 60). Third, both Paul and Seneca questioned traditional social hierarchies in light of their theology/philosophy. Fourth, we have no evidence that either of them condemned the institution of slavery as a whole.

SENECA'S *EPISTLE* 47

Lucius Annaeus Seneca was a Roman aristocrat and adherent to the ancient school of philosophy known as Stoicism. As a Stoic, he viewed the universe as a living organism created and providentially governed by a divine force called Reason, Fate, Zeus, or if one preferred, God; when providence appeared random (although in reality it was not), Reason could be referred to as Fortune. Present in everything, and most of all in humans, Reason constituted both a principle of order in accordance with which all things acted in harmony and a divine faculty through which people acted in agreement with this order. It was rational agreement with this order ("life in accordance with nature") that constituted good, and disagreement with this order ("life contrary to nature") that constituted bad. All other things—including health, financial circumstances, and social station—were matters of indifference.

The tension between "natural" status and "social" status inherent in the Stoic system is well illustrated in Seneca's discussion of slavery, to which he devotes his *Epistle* 47.[1] This discussion reveals some moderately countercultural tendencies, but also a great deal of social conservatism.

His opening comments represent the spirit of Stoicism well: "Do not think of these people as *slaves* but as *human beings*" (47.1, paraphrase).

---

[1]He wrote 124 epistles to his nephew Lucilius. These can be found in Seneca, *Epistles*, trans. Richard M. Gummere, LCL (London: Harvard University Press, 2006).

Undergirding Seneca's perspective is the Stoic conviction that God, or divine Reason, is present in all people equally. If it is the indwelling of divine Reason, above all, that makes one human, are slaves not also "human beings"? Of course, they are! And if one views slaves equally as "human beings" (see also 47.5) and social status as a matter of indifference, why not also view slaves even as, potentially, "friends"?

Seneca elaborates on these points throughout the letter. Masters must remember that all people stand on equal footing: "He whom you call your slave sprang from the same stock, is smiled upon by the same skies, and on equal terms with yourselves breathes, lives, and dies" (47.10). Seneca alludes here to the Stoic ideas that all people are offspring of God (*Ep.* 110.10), are cared for by God (*Ben.* 4.25.1–4.28.6), and ultimately suffer the same fate (*Ep.* 99.9).

The idea that people of every kind share the same "human" nature (the quality of *humanitas*) provides a philosophical basis for a Stoic version of the Golden Rule. Mutual recognition of each other *as people* creates the possibility of genuine sympathy, the ability to see oneself in another person and another person in oneself. Seneca applies this principle specifically to master-slave relations: "It is just as possible for you to see in him a free-born man as for him to see in you a slave" (47.10).

Noble birth was no sign of natural superiority, or low birth of natural inferiority. Is this not proved, Seneca asks, by the fact that social position sometimes changes? Those who have climbed nearly to the pinnacle of public honors, Fortune has thrown down from the precipice. The man on the path to the Senate-house has been knocked aside to the pasture (47.10). And the person who is now a master, Fortune may soon make a slave (47.12).[2] As Seneca points out in another letter, "Every king springs from a race of slaves, and every slave has had kings among his ancestors" (*Ep.* 44.3-4).

Therefore, one should judge slaves according to their character, not their social position (47.15-16). Elevate the slave to the master's table

---

[2]Did this not happen, Seneca asks, to Hecuba, to Croesus, Darius, Plato, and Diogenes?

if he is of worthy character. Invite another to the table not because he is worthy but so that he may *become* worthy (47.15). It does not matter if he is a slave—might he not have the soul of a freeman (47.17)?

Seneca levels the playing field not just by raising the slave to the level of the free, but also by reducing the free to the level of slaves. Slaves are "our fellow-slaves, if one reflects that Fortune has equal rights over slaves and free men alike." All people are slaves to something: "One is a slave to lust, another to greed, another to ambition, and all men are slaves to fear" (47.17). And moral slavery is much worse than social slavery (47.1)!

Although many masters opposed friendship with slaves, Seneca asks why they should *not* be counted as friends. Friends can be found not just among equals, but also among slaves (47.16). Let the slave talk with you, plan with you, live with you (47.13).

In other ways, Seneca's comments on slavery remain culturally conservative. While his censure to masters was grounded partly in morality, it was largely driven by practical concerns. He offers his advice as one of the ruling elite to other men of his class, with the aim not only of promoting the principles of his philosophy but also of helping masters maintain security from the threat of violence in the household, or still more serious, of slave uprising.

Masters would have less trouble with slaves, Seneca suggested, if they treated their slaves more humanely. Seneca describes with sadness the hardships they faced. While masters indulge themselves at their dinner parties until deep in the night, slaves are forced to stand on their feet, still and silent; masters whip their slaves even for coughing and hiccupping (47.2). What the guests cannot keep down after gorging themselves, the slaves mop up. The male servants are made to dress like women and to pluck their beards smooth, the better to satisfy their masters' lusts later in the evening. They treated their slaves dreadfully—what should masters expect? Indeed, slaves "are not enemies when we acquire them; we *make* them enemies" (47.5).

Even Seneca's warnings about the reversals of Fortune could be read primarily as a practical concern. Today you masters mistreat your slaves. Might you not one day become one? And how will some former slave treat you then? "Treat your inferiors as you would be treated by your betters" (47.11). As much as this bears a likeness to the Golden Rule, it stands also as an admonition that when the situation reverses, your former slave *will* treat you as you treated him (47.9). Master beware.

Despite putting masters and slaves on equal footing as "people," Seneca also reinforces traditional social inequalities. This version of the Golden Rule—"Treat your *inferiors* as you would be treated by your *betters*"—appears not to level the playing field, but works within the existing asymmetrical social structure. Seneca seems to have breathed in many commonplace social attitudes, and at moments breathed them back out apparently without filtering them through his Stoic grid. "'He is a slave.' His soul, however, may be that of a freeman" (47.17). This may appear to be a noble concession, but what is the "soul of a freeman"? Does this not correlate "social" status with "natural" status?

We find a similar example in the letter's climax. Just to be sure no one thinks that he is calling for the abolition of slavery, Seneca says plainly that he is not. Yes, slaves should "respect" their masters but not "fear" them (47.17), but this does not mean offering the "liberty-cap" to slaves in general. At this point Seneca grounds his view in a greater-to-lesser argument rooted in the hierarchy of nature: "What is enough for a *god* cannot be too little for a *master*" (47.18). In other words, *masters* are analogous to *God*, and *slaves* to *men*. This again maps *social* relationships (master-slave) onto *natural* ones (God-men). Seneca's point is that respect is something shown for friends of sorts, but still something directed at superiors.

In summary, Seneca's views on slavery are not without tension. Evidently he has no quarrel about the existence of slavery as an institution. He tells us that he is not calling for its abolition and, Stoic that he is, would tell us that the state of slavery itself is only a matter of indifference anyway. What mattered was that the slave lived a "life in agreement with nature," a moral life. On the other hand, for both philosophical and practical reasons, he had major concerns about common abuses of slaves and hence implored masters to treat slaves more humanely.

PAUL'S LETTER TO PHILEMON

The details behind Paul's letter to Philemon are hazy, but what can be gathered is this. Paul is in prison somewhere (probably in Rome or Ephesus). While in prison he encounters and converts a man named Onesimus (Philem 16), who happens to be a slave of a certain Philemon, whom Paul had also converted (Philem 19). Whether Onesimus had run away and encountered Paul by chance, or he had left his master's house in search of Paul, Onesimus seems to have done his master wrong, perhaps having made off with his money or property (Philem 18-19). Paul now sends Onesimus back to Philemon with the present letter in hand (Philem 12).

While the letter is far from a treatise on Paul's views on slavery, Paul's handling of the matter subtly reveals some of his thoughts on proper relationships between masters and slaves within the community of believers. Should their faith as Christians affect the way masters and slaves relate to each other? Should believers distinguish between their status as Christians and their status in society? Does their Christian status trump their social status?

Paul treads lightly, for it is a sensitive matter. He is noticeably reluctant to exert his apostolic authority. In most of his other letters,[3] he opens by describing himself as an "apostle" or elsewhere makes mention of his commissioning by God. Such a reference is conspicuously absent from his letter to Philemon. Instead he opens by calling himself a "prisoner of Christ Jesus" (Philem 1) and later states that although he has the "boldness" to issue commands, he, an "old man and prisoner," instead appeals to Philemon "on the basis of love" (Philem 8-9).

Paul does lay a certain claim to Onesimus. He had led the man to Christ ("my child, whom I begot"), and now he wishes to utilize his

---

[3]Philippians and 1–2 Thessalonians are the exceptions.

child's services (Philem 12). The exchange would only be fitting, since Philemon owes Paul a favor, and in fact, owes him his life (Philem 19). What was the cost of a slave in comparison with that? Still, Paul wants Philemon to extend the offer freely; he doesn't want to wrench Onesimus from his hands (Philem 13-14).

What kind of relationship Paul expects between the believing master and the now-believing slave Paul does not say, at least not in concrete terms. He takes an indirect approach. What he says is that, while Onesimus had been "useless" to Philemon as a slave, he has now become "useful," both to Paul and to Philemon (Philem 11), and that, while he and Philemon had been separated "for a little while," this happened so that Philemon could have Onesimus back "eternally," that is, as a "beloved brother" in the Lord (Philem 15-16).

Paul succeeds in being splendidly obscure. He is confident in Philemon's "obedience" (Philem 21), but in what does this "obedience" consist? In the whole matter, Paul has been speaking in riddles. What exactly does he want? Does he want to keep Onesimus for himself but still as a slave? Or does he desire Onesimus's services only after Philemon has freed him? Does he know what he wants?

The problem is more complex than it at first appears. There were macro issues. Slaves were essential to domestic life, to production, to education, to the military, to civic life, to the economy—indeed, to every domain of first-century social life in the Roman Empire. The problem also presented a conundrum on a micro-scale. What if the churches required Christian masters to free their slaves as a matter of policy? Slaves everywhere would clamor, "Sign me up! I'll be a Christian too!" It would quickly grow into an epidemic, at the risk not only of societal stability but also of the integrity of the church's membership.

It is of course possible that Paul abstained from ordering Onesimus's release because he found nothing immoral about Christian slavery. But this premise is questionable. Several details in the letter suggest that he viewed it as less than ideal in this case.

First, while more than one interpretation of Philemon 16 is possible (is Paul being intentionally ambiguous?), the phrasing seems peculiarly designed to point in the direction of freedom. That is, Paul does not say, "receive him *not only* as a slave *but also* a beloved brother"—which would point unequivocally toward retaining Onesimus as a slave—but rather, "receive him *no longer* as a slave but *more than* a slave, a beloved brother." This new relationship, Paul continues, holds not only "in the Lord" but also "in the flesh"; thus, Onesimus is presumably to be considered "no longer" a slave in either the Christian *or* the social domain of existence.

Second, Paul leaves comments throughout the letter that appear meaningful on their own, but that also fit together to form very suggestive configurations.

(a) If Paul and Philemon are "partners," and Philemon is to receive Onesimus as he would receive Paul (Philem 17), is Philemon not to accept Onesimus too as a "partner"?

(b) Paul says that Philemon once "refreshed" the "feelings" (*splagchna*) of the "*saints*" (Philem 7). He later describes Onesimus *as* his *own* heart, or literally as his "feelings" (*splagchna*). Finally in Philemon 20, he charges Philemon, "refresh *my* feelings" (*splagchna*). If Onesimus *is* Paul's "feelings," is this last remark code for "release Onesimus"?

(c) As Paul's own convert, Onesimus is his "son" in the faith (Philem 10); when Paul says that Philemon "owes" him his "life" (Philem 19), this almost undoubtedly means that Philemon too was his convert; if both Onesimus and Philemon are Paul's "sons," do they not stand on equal footing?

Each of these examples points toward the prospect of freedom only indirectly, but the logic seems evident.

Several points may be made about Paul's letter in conclusion. (1) Paul does not reject the prospect of the abolition of slavery, but neither does he raise the issue. (2) Paul does not address the legitimacy of slavery in general but rather a single case of Christian slavery. (3) Paul does not dictate orders to Philemon, but seeks to inspire him to action fitting in the Lord. (4) In addressing the letter not just "to Philemon," but "also to Apphia . . . and Archippus . . . and to *the church that meets in [his] home*" (Philem 1-2), Paul treats the issue not as an individual decision only, but as a community matter.

Conclusion

What do we gain as interpreters of Paul by setting his views on slavery next to Seneca's? One outcome of this juxtaposition is that it illustrates how deeply cultural context shapes perspectives in a particular setting. One might expect Paul's Christian faith to have moved him to political activism in opposition to the institution of slavery. But this expectation owes a lot to our modern context, rather than to Paul's own context. We view the issue of slavery today from a post-abolitionist perspective, when the general consensus of Western society is that slavery is morally wrong. But to a person in a context where the institution was still well established and its legitimacy widely accepted, this view would not have occurred as obvious. Attention to the writings of Seneca further demonstrate this point, that if Seneca could *deny* that his philosophy demanded an end to slavery even when it *appeared to do so* (by his admission in 47.17-18), arguably it was because the social outlook of the times considered the possibility of abolition, and even the need for it, as literally out of the question.

On another level, the comparison illustrates that Christians were not *in all respects* unique. Non-Christians, especially advocates of the ancient philosophies, advocated for better treatment of slaves on moral grounds, just as Paul did.

Yet a close reading of Paul's letter to Philemon and Seneca's forty-seventh epistle also reveals a subtle difference in their stances on the legitimacy of slavery as such. Informed by Stoicism, Seneca was able to maintain the legitimacy of slavery and even to explicitly deny the need for abolition on the basis that social rank was a matter of moral "indifference." Paul, by contrast, gestured toward the inappropriateness of the master-slave relationship—at least in the case of fellow-believers Philemon and Onesimus—on the basis that they had become "brothers" in Christ. Whether Paul meant to gesture all the way to abolition is a difficult question, one that cannot be decided on the basis of this text alone.

For Further Reading

Primary Sources

Seneca. *Epistles.* Translated by Richard M. Gummere. LCL. London: Harvard University Press, 2006.

———. *Moral Essays.* Translated by John W. Basore. LCL. London: Harvard University Press, 2003.

Secondary Sources

Barclay, J. M. G. "Paul, Philemon and the Dilemma of Christian Slave-Ownership." *NTS* 37 (1991): 161-86.

Baraz, Yelena. "True Greatness of Soul in Seneca's *De Constantia Sapientis.*" In *Roman Reflections,* edited by Gareth D. Williams and Katharina Volk, 157-71, Studies in Latin Philosophy. Oxford: Oxford University Press, 2016.

Bartchy, S. S. "Response to Keith Bradley's Scholarship on Slavery." *BibInt* 21 (2013): 524-32.

Bradley, K. R. "Seneca and Slavery." In *Seneca,* edited by John G. Fitch, 335-47, Oxford Readings in Classical Studies. Oxford: Oxford University Press, 2008. Reprint of "Seneca and Slavery." *C&M* 37 (1986): 161-72.

Brookins, Timothy A. "'I Rather Appeal to *Auctoritas*': Roman Conceptualizations of Power and Paul's Letter to Philemon." *CBQ* 77 (2015): 302-21.

———. "(Dis)correspondence of Paul and Seneca on Slavery." In *Paul and Seneca in Dialogue,* edited by Joseph R. Dodson and David E. Briones, 179-207. Ancient Philosophy and Religion 2. Leiden: Brill, 2017.

Byron, John. *Recent Research on Paul and Slavery.* Recent Research in Biblical Studies 3. Sheffield: Sheffield Phoenix, 2008.

Garnsey, P. D. A. *Ideas of Slavery from Aristotle to Augustine.* Cambridge: Cambridge University Press, 1996.

Griffin, Miriam T. "Seneca on Slavery." In *Seneca: A Philosopher in Politics,* 256-85. Oxford: Oxford University Press, 1976.

Martin, Dale. *Slavery as Salvation.* New Haven, CT: Yale University Press, 1990.

Peterson, Norman R. *Rediscovering Paul: Philemon and the Sociology of Paul's Narrative World.* Philadelphia: Fortress, 1985. Reprint, Wipf and Stock, 2008.

Discussion Questions

1. Do you think that sharing a common nature as human beings makes it mandatory that all people share the same status in society, i.e., the same "social status"?

2. Would it be possible for social hierarchies to exist in a Christian utopia?

3. Do you think that Seneca's views on slavery were consistent? Do you think that Paul's views were consistent? Why or why not?

4. Would it bother you if Paul viewed Christian slavery as legitimate? Why or why not?

5

ALL FOR ONE AND ONE FOR ALL

INDIVIDUAL AND COMMUNITY IN PAUL AND EPICTETUS

BEN C. DUNSON

Many observers of modern Western societies have noted that community life—civic groups, bowling leagues, book clubs, and the like—is decaying. Our communities are becoming more and more individualistic, and we're worse off because of it. Many argue that rampant consumerist individualism has harmed society severely. Similarly, it has been noted that certain strands of Christian theology can give the impression that Christianity is simply about "me, myself, and Jesus" and nothing more. One sociologist, Robert Putnam, has memorably described America today using the image of the sad ten-pin bowler—bowling alone—increasingly unable to find stability and meaning in life. Why? Because that sort of support can only be found within community structures that are rapidly disappearing in the West. In response to Putnam's dismal portrayal of modern life, diverse streams of thought, ranging from Marxist political theory to modern sociology and psychology, have vigorously protested the evils of present-day individualism. As a result, a focus on community has increasingly begun to dominate almost every realm of the human sciences over the last half-century, including the study of the apostle Paul.

In this chapter, I will demonstrate how the individual and community figure prominently in the writings of the apostle Paul and the Stoic philosopher Epictetus in similar ways. But I will also show fundamental differences between the two when they articulate the exact *way* in which the individual and community stand in relation to one another.

INDIVIDUAL AND COMMUNITY IN EPICTETUS: SELF-PRESERVATION AND SOCIETY

To understand why Epictetus describes the nature of human individuality in the way that he does, one must first understand some things about his ethical system. And in order to understand his ethical system, one must first understand that for him (and almost all ancient philosophers) ethics is about the pursuit of happiness (understood not as selfish indulgence but as holistic well-being). In short, happiness comes about by living virtuously, in harmony with nature. And Epictetus believes his philosophy of life can secure happiness for his followers, no matter what circumstances they face in life. In fact, that is the most distinctive and significant feature of his whole philosophical system.

Epictetus lays out his plan for happiness in many sections of his lectures. He does this perhaps nowhere more clearly and succinctly than in *Discourse* 2.8. Here we read that the good life consists in a "desire that is always achievable, the certainty of avoiding what is undesired, choosing what is appropriate, a thoughtful plan, a carefully considered agreement" (*Disc.* 2.8.29). There is a lot going on in this compact statement, but essentially Epictetus is telling his students that unshakable happiness is found solely in those things that one cannot fail to obtain, in those things that are "under our control" (see *Disc.* 1.22.10). Our happiness is not tied to the presence of positive external circumstances (see *Disc.* 1.4.1-4). Contrary to how our modern world thinks, happiness isn't found in the next big move, in getting a promotion, or in entering into a new relationship. And it can't be taken away by economic hardship, losing a job, or getting rejected by someone. It lies in something more stable than that. Epictetus uses the term "moral purpose" (see *Disc.* 3.2.13) to describe the individual's inborn decision-making power to focus only on one's own virtue, which is under one's control, rather than to let oneself be influenced and overwhelmed by external circumstances, which are not under our control. Our moral purpose, in other words, is like what we mean today when we speak of "moral compass" or "conscience." It is that internal voice telling us to do the right thing, and for Epictetus, making sure we do not become slaves to circumstance. In essence, if our lives are dependent on how things are going outwardly, then our happiness will always be under threat, subject to chance and the whims of fortune. But if it has to do with things that are under our control, our happiness now becomes secure and stable.

What does this have to do with the nature of the human person, with the relation of individuals and community? Put simply, people can only be absolutely sure that they will find happiness if they center their moral purpose on themselves and their own mental states, since everything else lies outside of their powers. The goal of happiness—the goal of Epictetus's entire philosophical system, which is synonymous with virtue—can be secured in no other way than through the effort of the individual on his or her own. Ethics, by definition, is (and must be) centered on the individual, at least in this foundational sense.

However, for Epictetus, this focus on the individual is not at odds with a focus on community or social responsibility. A good example of this is seen in *Discourse* 2.22, where Epictetus sets out how he sees his individualistic moral teaching cohering with a concern for the well-being of others. *Discourse* 2.22 is a lengthy lecture titled "On Friendship" that begins with a thematic statement describing the impulse that drives all human action: "Whatever a man is interested in he naturally loves" (*Disc.* 2.22.1). After discussing reasons for confusion about friendship (*Disc.* 2.22.1-3) and why purely natural affection for other people is a weak ground for true camaraderie (*Disc.* 2.22.4-14), Epictetus restates the "general rule" or universal truth of human relationships: "that every living creature has no concern greater than its own interest" (*Disc.* 2.22.15). In fact, as the next sentence affirms, self-interest entirely determines the objects of one's love and desire, being of necessity more important than our love for even our friends and family, whom we will spurn if they get in the way of our happiness (*Disc.* 2.22.16).

At the outset of this lecture, then—despite its title—it sounds as if there is no place at all for friendship and other-regarding attitudes in Epictetus's ethical system. However, beginning in *Discourse* 2.22.18, Epictetus transitions from speaking of this all-controlling, self-preservative impulse to the way in which it touches on one's relationships with other people. To do this, Epictetus maintains that a person has two options. Either one's family and friends are placed together with one's self-interest, or they are treated as separate goods in competition with personal interest.

What he means by this is clarified in *Discourse* 2.22.19-21. First, he insists that humans will always be inclined toward what they perceive as best for themselves. This is stated memorably in *Discourse* 2.22.19: "Where there is an 'I' or a 'mine,' there a creature must incline." Second, there are only three options as to where human desire can be directed: bodily urges, moral purpose, or external things, that is, anything that is outside of oneself or one's own control. External things could include things as mundane as the weather or as significant as one's job or family. Whichever of these three things captures one's desires reveals the location of the "ruling power" of the individual's life (*Disc.* 2.22.19). The ruling power of a person's life is that which dominates their thoughts and time, that which fundamentally shapes their lives. Most people get caught up in living to satisfy their bodily urges and are constantly anxious about the external things happening to them. However, only the moral purpose (moral compass, conscience) is actually able to guarantee right living, social or otherwise.

As Epictetus argues repeatedly throughout the *Discourses*, one's moral purpose is the center of human thought and action, and must be vigorously trained to seek only what it should. And what it should seek is to be totally content with whatever outward circumstances one encounters in life. In this particular instance, as Epictetus states in *Discourse* 2.22.20, only when the ruling power is under the control of one's moral purpose is it possible to relate properly to other people (see also *Disc.* 2.22.27). That is to say, only if a person seeks to preserve his or her own virtue and to attend exclusively to that which he needs to be concerned with (morally speaking) will such a person "be the friend and son and the father that he should be" (*Disc.* 2.22.20). Consequently, self-interest and a sincere care for others are merged into a single and unified impulse; the individual and community come together. Care for others is actually folded into self-interest, which then leads one to seek to "preserve [one's] relations" (*Disc.* 22.20). Maintaining your personal virtue leads you to maintain (as much as it is up to you) good relationships with other people. The potential for conflict between personal well-being and communal well-being, therefore, disappears (at least in theory).

Even so, relationships with others can never become goods in and of themselves. That would mean finding your happiness in external things subject to possibly adverse circumstances rather than things under your control. It is true that Epictetus does not do away with the community when promoting individual self-interest as the main impulse of life. Yet, he does relativize social relationships by placing them within the sphere of personal self-interest. Family ties and friendships, for Epictetus, are "external things" that cannot guarantee happiness, since they are outside of one's own control. We should pursue harmony in these relationships, but only because we are pursuing our own virtue, thus focusing on something we can actually control. Ironically, then, seeking the well-being of others as a good in itself destroys the very possibility of true social responsibility, because such well-being becomes dependent on something external. Alternatively, communal faithfulness is assuredly preserved if—*and only if*—one sets his or her self-interest solely on one's own moral purpose, which alone aligns with the moral point of view of the universe (*Disc.* 22.27-30).

In sum, the focus on self-interest in Epictetus's ethics is pointedly individualistic, a word that instinctively causes many modern readers to recoil. (If by "individualistic," modern, Western individualism is meant, we are right to reject the term. But the word does in fact capture the essence of his approach quite well.) For Epictetus, ethical behavior is based firmly on seeking self-benefit through self-control and mental discipline. Yet, at the same time, he doesn't allow the individual component of his philosophical approach to eclipse the social component. The individual self has priority, but it is a priority that forms a foundation for the well-being and harmony of all of one's social relationships.

INDIVIDUAL AND COMMUNITY IN PAUL: FAITH AND FELLOWSHIP

Although Epictetus prioritizes the self-sufficient individual, he also incorporates a concern for others into his philosophical system. Paul has a similar approach. He, too, believes that the individual is not at odds with the community. However, differences emerge when we consider the way Paul integrates a concern for others into his understanding of the individual. His emphasis on community ends up being much more central than it is in Epictetus's teaching. This truth can be seen in many ways, but we will focus on one: what Paul says about "faith" in his letter to the Christians in Rome.

Interpreters of Romans have traditionally spoken of faith as an individual action. Although debates have raged ever since the Protestant Reformation about what exactly Paul is talking about in Romans 1:16-17, it is clear that faith is at the heart of it. Faith, in fact, runs like a thread through the entire letter of Romans, dominating Romans 3:21–5:2 and then resurfacing repeatedly throughout chapters 9–12, as well as in chapter 14.

But what is faith? There is certainly no shortage of answers to this question, especially in more recent times.[1] In our attempt to answer this question, we could do no better than turn to Paul's most explicit teaching on faith in the letter, Romans 9–10.

For Paul, there are two ways to be right with God. Put simply, you can be right with God either by doing what God says or by believing in Jesus Christ. We see this most clearly in Romans 10:5-13. Moses "writes about the righteousness that is based on the law, that the person who does the commandments shall live by them" (Rom 10:5

---

[1]See, for example, Jeanette Hagen Pifer's chapter in this volume, "Don't Stop Believing."

ESV, quoting from Lev 18:5). Keep the law, and righteousness will be yours. But there is another path to righteousness, and that is a good thing, considering that Paul says in Romans 3:20 that "by works of the law no human being will be justified in his sight." What is this other path? Paul tells us in Romans 10:6-10:

> The righteousness based on faith says, "Do not say in your heart, 'Who will ascend into heaven?'" (that is, to bring Christ down) "or 'Who will descend into the abyss?'" (that is, to bring Christ up from the dead). But what does it say? "The word is near you, in your mouth and in your heart" (that is, the word of faith that we proclaim); because, if you confess with your mouth that Jesus is Lord and believe in your heart that God raised him from the dead, you will be saved. For with the heart one believes and is justified, and with the mouth one confesses and is saved. (ESV)

In these verses, Paul reads Deuteronomy 30:12-14 in light of Christ's work of redemption to argue that the only way to be saved and justified (declared righteous) is by believing in Jesus Christ. Being righteous in God's sight, paradoxically, does not come from pursuing and attaining one's own righteousness by keeping God's law (as Israel unsuccessfully attempted [Rom 9:31–10:3]), but simply by trusting (believing) in Jesus Christ. He is "the end of the law for righteousness to everyone who believes" (Rom 10:4 ESV), which is simply to say that Jesus is the only way an unrighteous person (see Rom 3:10-20) can be declared righteous in the eyes of a righteous God (see Rom 3:21-26).

Throughout Romans 10:6-17, only second and third person singular verbs are used to describe the actions of faith and confession, as well as the righteousness and salvation that result from faith. In short, every *individual* person "who believes in him will not be put to shame" (Rom 10:11 ESV, quoting Is 28:16); every *individual* person "who calls on the name of the Lord will be saved" (Rom 10:13 ESV, quoting Joel 2:32). Faith, quite clearly, is something that an individual must possess in order to be saved; it is the very means of taking hold of the divine gift of salvation.

Is Paul, then, just as centered on self-preservation as Epictetus? In short, no. Faith, which is (and must be) the disposition of the individual who would be saved, is not *merely* an individual thing. Even in chapter 10 faith is more than a merely individualistic endeavor:

> If you confess with your mouth that Jesus is Lord and believe in your heart that God raised him from the dead, you will be saved. For with the heart one believes and is justified, and with the mouth one confesses and is saved. (Rom 10:9-10 ESV)

Confession is an inherently public and social act. You don't confess your faith to and for yourself. You confess before the world and the believing community. But the social and communal dimension of faith becomes even more evident in Romans 12.

Romans 12 is a critical point of transition in the letter. Although Paul has already touched on the believer's necessary obedience to God previously in the letter, a pronounced shift to ethical exhortation begins in Romans 12:1. In this verse, Paul appeals to the Roman Christians "by the mercies of God," that is, by all he has already written about God's grace to them in Christ, to "present your bodies as a living sacrifice, holy and acceptable to God, which is your spiritual worship." Christians, although living as individuals ("bodies"), are to offer up the entirety of their lives to God as a single "living sacrifice." Just as the burnt offering in the Old Testament was completely consumed by fire, so too must their lives be completely consumed in their devotion and service to the Lord. The fact that this sacrifice is a singular noun is critical. It proves that an isolated Christian—living for the self, outside of the community of believers—is not only foolish, but impossible.

This impossibility is central to Paul's thought as he continues in Romans 12:3—his exhortation to each believer that he is not to "think of himself more highly than he ought to think." Instead, he must think of himself "with sober judgment," which is simply a way of saying that the believer must see him- or herself in the proper perspective, rather than exalting the self above others within the believing community.

How is this possible? Paul tells us in the latter half of verse 3: a believer can think with sober (or correct, undeceived) judgment by using "the measure of faith that God has assigned" to each believer.

Some see this "measure of faith" as an objective standard given to all believers to provide them with a proper estimation of their place in God's church. Others insist that it is a unique gift, a portion of faith given in larger measure to some, and smaller measure to others. I lean toward the first of these interpretations, which means that the measure of faith (the measure that consists in faith) is like a ruler or a measuring cup. The faith believers possess is the standard by which they can think rightly about themselves in relation to fellow believers within the community of God's people. What, then, does rightly using this measure of faith lead to? Paul argues that it *should* cause the believer to meditate on the fact that he or she is merely a single "member" within the "one body" of Jesus Christ (Rom 12:4). Within this body each member has a different function, so that multiplicity takes a backseat to unity within the "one body in Christ" (Rom 12:5 ESV). By grace, each member has a distinctive spiritual gift from God, which should be used in service to him, instead of leading to jealous comparisons and resentful rivalries (Rom 12:6-8).

Faith, then, has an indispensably community-building function. Equipped with their new faith-fashioned thinking (the measure of faith), believers are able to see that a diversity of functions and gifts within the body of Christ is not a problem to be overcome, but a divine gift to be celebrated. The resulting principle of diversity-within-unity then serves as a bridge that introduces the large sections of moral imperatives stretching from 12:9 to 15:13, commands focused primarily on love, harmony, and peacefulness within the community of believers. Paul captures this dynamic well in Romans 14:7 (ESV) when he says that "none of us lives to himself, and none of us dies to himself." Faith's role in all of this is then restated in Romans 14:23 ESV: "whatever does not proceed from faith is sin." Faith is—or at least is meant to be—a powerful force at work among the Roman believers to unify them in heart and mind for their common task of worshipping God and serving one another. This common faith, as becomes clear in chapters 12–15, is a spiritual gift (see also Rom 1:11) given for the edification of the entire community and not simply for the salvation of the individual. Here too, however, Paul appeals to each specific *individual* in Romans 12:3 to put his or her individual gifts to use in service to the single body.

The goal of Paul's mission is to bring about the "obedience of faith" among all the nations of the world, a phrase that bookends Romans (see Rom 1:5; 16:26 ESV). This phrase likely has a double meaning: faith, or trust in Jesus Christ for salvation, is itself an act of individual obedience and submission to God, but faith necessarily also brings about a lifestyle of obedience in those who have been saved. This "obedience that flows from faith," then, will always be at work among God's people, bringing together the many members of the body of Christ so that they are made into the singular sacrifice Paul writes of in Romans 12:1.

Faith in Romans, then, is about how individuals are saved, but it is not only that. Faith is also the glue that binds and unites every believer in self-sacrificial love and service. The individual and the community are joined together in an unbreakable bond.

CONCLUSION

What, then, can be said about Paul and Epictetus on the individual and community? For Epictetus, the individual self has an absolute primacy that cannot be compromised without at the same time jeopardizing a fundamental tenet of his philosophy, namely, that nothing external—including social relations—may be allowed to determine one's happiness. At the same time, he insists that self-mastery will lead to virtue, which itself leads to care for others. But if you get it backwards the whole system comes crashing down: by turning care for others into a good in itself, you become dependent on things outside your control; by becoming dependent on things outside your control you destroy the possibility of attaining to virtue no matter the circumstances.

The apostle Paul, too, believes that the individual and community must be linked together. His way of doing this, however, is different than Epictetus's, and quite substantially so. For Paul, the individual believer is *necessarily* embodied within the body of all believers, which is the body of Christ. Paul does not share Epictetus's worry about external things affecting us. In fact, Paul believes that many external things *should* affect us. The plight of fellow believers, for example, should impact us deeply. Believers are bound to the well-being of other believers; they are debtors to one another: "Owe no one anything, except to love each other" (Rom 13:8 ESV; cf. Rom 15:1). If one suffers, all suffer; if one rejoices all rejoice (Rom 12:15). Because of his teaching on self-sufficiency, such a notion would have been troubling to Epictetus. In contrast, it lies at the heart of Paul's theology because in all of his teaching he looks to Christ, first as savior, then as example: "For Christ did not please himself, but as it is written 'The reproaches of those who reproached you fell on me'" (Rom 15:3). Being a Christian *means* living a life united with the lives of fellow believers, because it means living together in union with Jesus Christ. In the church, it is all for one and one for all with no place for lone-ranger Christians.

SIMILARITIES AND DIFFERENCES

Table 5.1. Similarities and differences

Epictetus, *Of Friendship* (*Discourse* 22)	Paul, *The Letter to the Romans*
Love of others is based on self-interest.	Love of others is based on gratitude for the love received from Jesus Christ.
Only the wise person has the power to love others.	Wisdom leads to discerning God's will, which in turn leads one to love others.
One must never act because of an external obligation. Love must be chosen as an act of will.	Love of others is a divine obligation placed upon a believer in Jesus Christ, but it is empowered by divine grace.
Virtue may demand a seeming sympathy with those experiencing hardship, but one must never allow one's self to be inwardly moved by the plight of others, since this is a circumstance outside of one's own control.	Love necessarily leads to genuine sympathy for others who are experiencing hardship.
The power to love others resides entirely within one's own power of volition (moral purpose).	The power to love others truly is a gift of God's mercy.

For Further Reading

Primary Sources

Epictetus. *Discourses, Books I–II.* Translated by W. A. Oldfather. LCL. Cambridge, MA: Harvard University Press, 1925.

———. *Discourses, Books III–IV, The Encheiridion.* Translated by W. A. Oldfather. LCL. Cambridge, MA: Harvard University Press, 1928.

Secondary Sources

Barclay, John M. G. "Security and Self-Sufficiency: A Comparison of Paul and Epictetus." *ExAud* 24 (2008): 60-72.

Bonhöffer, Adolf. *The Ethics of the Stoic Epictetus.* Translated by William O. Stephens. Revisioning Philosophy 2. New York: Peter Lang, 1997.

Dunson, Ben C. "Faith in Romans: The Salvation of the Individual or Life in Community?" *JSNT* 34, no. 1 (2011): 19-46.

———. *Individual and Community in Paul's Letter to the Romans.* WUNT 2/332. Tübingen: Mohr Siebeck, 2012.

———. "The Individual and Community in Twentieth and Twenty-first-Century Pauline Scholarship." *CurBR* 9 (2010): 63-97

Eastman, Susan Grove. *Paul and the Person: Reframing Paul's Anthropology.* Grand Rapids: Eerdmans, 2017.

Engberg-Pedersen, Troels. "The Relationship with Others: Similarities and Differences Between Paul and Stoicism." *ZNW* 96 (2005): 35-60.

Esler, Philip F. "Paul and Stoicism: Romans 12 as a Test Case." *NTS* 50 (2004): 106-24.

Long, A. A. *Epictetus: A Stoic and Socratic Guide to Life.* Oxford: Oxford University Press, 2002.

Malherbe, Abraham J. "Paul's Self-Sufficiency (Philippians 4:11)." In *Friendship, Flattery, and Frankness of Speech: Studies on Friendship in the New Testament World,* edited by J. T. Fitzgerald, NovTSup 82. Leiden: Brill, 1996.

Reydams-Schils, Gretchen. *The Roman Stoics: Self, Responsibility, and Affection.* Chicago: University of Chicago Press, 2005.

Discussion Questions

1. In what ways do Epictetus and Paul help you understand how genuinely to care for others?

2. Does self-interest give you a sufficient foundation for caring for other people (as Epictetus argues it does)?

3. Must we abandon the whole idea of individual identity in order to care for others?

4. What difference does grounding our love of others in the mercy we have already received from God make in how we view our relationships with other people?

6

DON'T STOP BELIEVING

PAUL AND PLUTARCH ON FAITH

JEANETTE HAGEN PIFER

THE CONCEPT OF FAITH IN OUR MODERN WORLD varies widely depending on different cultural, religious, and intellectual contexts. For some, faith indicates a hopeful disposition toward something when knowledge is lacking. For example, one might have faith that she will win the lottery even though there is no logical or factual basis for this "belief." For others, faith is confidence in something based on experience. We express this kind of faith all the time. When we sit on a chair, we believe (based on past experiences) that the chair will hold our weight.

When the apostle Paul refers to faith, he means something rather specific, yet comprehensive and distinctive. Pauline faith is, of course, rooted in knowledge about Jesus Christ, but is it mere conjecture and hopeful optimism? Or does Paul convey something much more secure? Before we unpack what Paul means by faith, it is helpful to explore the understanding of faith among Greco-Roman philosophers in the ancient world.

FAITH IN GRECO-ROMAN PHILOSOPHICAL TRADITION

In the Greco-Roman world as well as in Hellenistic Judaism, the words *pistis* (Greek) and *fides* (Latin), both translated as "faith" or "belief" in English, were quite common and could be translated in many ways. Fortunately, the varied definitions can be categorized in two general ways: *rational* and *relational*. On a very basic level, the rational understanding of *pistis/fides* depicts faith or belief as hopeful optimism. In other words, this use of *pistis* referred to a confidence in something else, whether an idea, a person, relationship, or thing, but it did not indicate absolute certainty. For example, the pre-Platonic philosopher, Sophocles (5th century BC), writes: "My faith extends so far, that I can believe it, but I have never put it to the test" (*Trachiniae* 588-93).[1] Here, faith accepts something as true without requiring evidence.

Understood this way, it makes sense that philosophers began to regard faith as an intellectually weak way of relating to the world. By the fourth century BC, Plato writes of the inferiority and instability of *pistis*. In *The Republic*, Plato describes four conditions in the soul, from highest to lowest: understanding, thought, belief, and imagination (511e and 534a). In this hierarchy, *pistis* is just a shadow of knowledge, a less stable state of soul (505d-e).

Evidence of this understanding of belief as an inferior mental state persists through the third century AD. Plotinus speaks of belief as a sort of naive acceptance of phenomena. In the *Enneads* (III.6.6.67), Plotinus reproaches those who find their "faith [*pistis*] of truth" in the "apparitions which come by way of sense-perception."[2] Here *pistis* is used pejoratively of an unreasoned acceptance of things sensed, but not substantiated reality.

At times *pistis* is used with more rhetorical force to indicate a pledge, guarantee, or evidence. Plato and Aristotle use the term in this way in their developments of the art of rhetorical persuasion. Aristotle in his treatise *Rhetoric* explains that *pistis* is used to persuade (1.11). The word can be translated as a "convincing argument" or "means of conviction." Plato uses *pistis* specifically to refer to a strong argument, or proof, for the immortality of the soul (*Phaedo* 70B). In the context of speaking about love, Plato employs *pistis* to refer to a pledge of friendship (*Phaedo* 256D). As you can see, among

---

[1]Unless otherwise noted, all translations of Greek and Latin texts are taken from the Loeb editions.
[2]The Loeb translation translates *pistis* here as "guarantee."

Greco-Roman philosophers, *pistis* was used with a wide range of meanings within the rational category, from wishful thinking to logical and reasoned evidence.

Under the *relational* category, *pistis* and *fides* were used widely to describe the trust that is foundational to all relationships. For example, Cicero writes that *pistis* "is the unswerving constancy, which we look for in friendship" (*De Amicitia* 65). Epictetus likewise writes about the importance of keeping "good faith" toward fathers and sons alike (*Discourses* 2.22.18-20). *Pistis/fides* in the master-slave relationship was also regarded as critical. Valerius Maximus writes of the mutual fidelity between a man, C. Plotius Plancus, and his slaves. After Plancus had been condemned by the Triumvirs, his slaves refused to reveal his whereabouts, even being willing to die on his behalf. When Plancus observed such steadfast fidelity, he turned himself in to the soldiers in order to save the lives of his slaves. Valerius concludes: "Such a contest of mutual well-wishing makes it hard to determine which was the more deserving: the master to find such steadfast fidelity in his slaves or the slaves to be freed from the cruelty of interrogation by their master's just compassion" (*Memorable Doings and Sayings* 6.8.5).

Often, *pistis* indicates faithfulness or reliability, especially in its use by the Stoics. Epictetus, for example, posits that man is born to fidelity and remarks how shameful it is for the man who abandons such faithfulness (*Disc.* 2.4.1). Indeed, infidelity breeds a whole host of consequences such as the loss of self-respect, piety, as well as friendship and all other relationships. He compares the unfaithful person to a wasp who is not only deemed worthless, but will be struck down by others because of the pain he causes.

Finally, *pistis/fides* was used to depict the relationship between god and humans. In this relationship, both the rational and relational aspects of faith are often implied. For Apollonius of Tyana, *pistis* toward the gods reflected an essential aspect in the most important of all relationships (*Letters* 33). Philo of Alexandria also uses *pistis* in the relational sense of trusting in God (*On Flight and Finding* 152) along with the rational understanding of *pistis* as evidence or proof (*On Flight and Finding* 136; *On Abraham* 141).

Table 6.1. Rational and relational

Rational	It refers to the varying degrees of confidence in something else, whether an idea, a person, relationship, or thing, but it did not indicate absolute certainty.
Relational	Describes the trust that is foundational to all relationships, indicating faithfulness or reliability—including that between god and humans.

PLUTARCH ON FAITH

With this broad overview of the range of meanings of *pistis* and *fides* in Greco-Roman philosophy, we will take a closer look at one philosopher, Plutarch, who was a contemporary of Paul. Our examination here will help to set the stage for our discussion of what makes Paul's concept of faith distinctive. Plutarch utilized *pistis* frequently in a variety of ways, both rational and relational. From the rational standpoint, Plutarch relays a dialogue in *Amatorius* in which one character demands proofs for belief in the gods while another character admonishes him that their ancient, traditional faith is sufficient. For Plutarch, the tradition of faith is the foundation of religion.

Plutarch also employs *pistis* to convey trustworthiness in a variety of human-to-human relationships. For example, he writes of the trustworthiness of statesmen (*Moralia* 539e-f; 1129c) and warns against trusting those who break truces (*Caesar* 22.2). He also uses it in a basic religious sense of belief and/or disbelief in the gods along with associated religious customs and outcomes (*Moralia* 359f-60b). This usage carries both rational and relational elements.

In his treatise *Superstition*, Plutarch argues that "ignorance and blindness in regard to the gods divides itself at the very beginning into two streams," either atheism or superstition (1e). For Plutarch, atheism leads to an indifference in life while superstition reflects an emotional assumption that produces crushing fear that the gods will inflict pain (2b-c). He concludes that atheism is falsified reason and superstition is an emotion arising from false reason (2c). Religious faith for Plutarch is the more reasonable basis for living life.

Specific to his view of faith in relation to the gods, Plutarch follows Plato in the idea that the divine is the exemplar of every virtue, and that the goal of the human is to follow god (*Moralia* 550d). Humans can acquire virtues, including *pistis*, by imitating the god who not only is a pattern for virtue, but also embodies every virtue himself (Plutarch, *Moralia* 550d; quoting Plato, *Theaetetus* 176e).

PAUL ON FAITH IN 1 CORINTHIANS

Paul's rational faith. Paul's understanding of faith, having some points of similarity, extends far beyond the Greco-Roman philosophical tradition that we have just examined. At the rational level, faith for Paul is definitely not just hopeful optimism when knowledge is inaccessible. It is confident assurance in the foundational tenets of Christianity. The best example of the rational aspects of faith in Paul is found in 1 Corinthians 15, where he clearly presents the fundamental elements of the gospel. While focusing on the centrality of Christ's resurrection, Paul outlines the objective aspects of faith: (1) Christ died for our sins according to the Scriptures, (2) he was buried, and (3) he was raised on the third day (1 Cor 15:3-4).

For Paul, these claims are neither baseless nor wishful thinking. He is not inviting naive people to adopt a blind faith. There is reason to trust in this gospel, and Paul forcefully reminds his readers of this, confirming his claims with a detailed account of eyewitnesses. Verses 5-8 list the appearances of the resurrected Christ to Cephas, the twelve, over five hundred brothers at one time, James, and to Paul himself.

Paul argues for the reality of the resurrection in the verses that follow as well. In verse 12, Paul contests those who have rejected a general resurrection of the dead (1 Cor 15:12), and he proceeds to outline the outcome of such a denial. If there is no resurrection then not even Christ has been raised (1 Cor 15:13). And if Christ had not been raised, Paul's preaching is in vain and their faith is in vain (1 Cor 15:14, 17). Not only that, but Paul is found to be a liar (1 Cor 15:15), the Corinthians are still in their sins (1 Cor 15:17), those who are asleep "in Christ" have perished (1 Cor 15:18), and they of all people are most to be pitied (1 Cor 15:19).

Both here and in his gospel proclamation earlier (1 Cor 15:2), Paul repeats a warning against vain faith using three different but related words: *eikē* (1 Cor 15:2), *kenos* (1 Cor 15:14), and *mataios* (1 Cor 15:17). *Eikē* is defined as pertaining to there being no cause, nor reason, nor purpose. *Kenos* can refer to something being materially or metaphorically empty. *Mataios* likewise means pertaining to being of no use, empty, fruitless. Each word conveys the idea that belief in Christ with no objective basis in the resurrection is futile. Without the resurrection, faith is empty, without substance or content, and thus meaningless. Yet, having laid a foundation for faith in the resurrection through his list of eyewitnesses, we see that for Paul, faith is grounded in and founded upon an event that really happened.

Paul's relational faith. While Paul's view of faith does involve a rational agreement with truth claims, it carries with it all of the relational components evident in the Greco-Roman philosophical tradition, and more. To demonstrate the relational components of faith, we will look at 1 Corinthians 1:26–2:5 and then again at 1 Corinthians 15:1-2. We will look at the ways in which Paul uses the term *pistis* and investigate other terminology and metaphors that he uses that might explain what he means by faith.

In 1 Corinthians 1:26-31 and 2:1-5, Paul presents two lines of argumentation using two terms, "boasting" (1 Cor 1:31) and "faith" (1 Cor 2:5), to describe the only acceptable human attitude before God. The similarity of structure and conceptual continuity in the two passages suggests that Paul uses the two words in similar ways. In other words, "boasting" illuminates in part what he means by "faith." In the first passage, Paul reveals the Corinthians' vain quest for wisdom, power, and prestige in order to underscore that all worldly forms of worth are made null by the power of the gospel (1 Cor 1:26-31). The natural human tendency is self-exaltation, self-confidence, and even self-sufficiency. Yet Paul argues that these tendencies are contrary to true gospel living. No human being can rightfully boast in the presence of God (1 Cor 1:29).

Paul's use of the term "boasting" in his correspondence with the Corinthians is understandable when considered alongside the key themes Paul addresses as well as the cultural and historical context of first-century Greco-Roman society. At the time of Paul's writing, Corinth was growing to be one of the largest and most prosperous cities in Greece, with a government that was set up to reflect the earlier Republican era. There was a zeal for the growing civic and individual boasting that has been documented and preserved in inscriptions describing individuals' charitable contributions, achievements, or societal status. Interestingly, these inscriptions were often self-funded, confirming that self-promotion was common in Corinthian culture.

It is in this context of a city noted for its wealth, with citizens striving after power and fame, that Paul appeals to Jeremiah's admonition against boasting in their own resources. Instead, the right focus of boasting is this: "Let the one who boasts, boast in the Lord" (1 Cor 1:30-31 ESV; cf. Jer 9:23-24). It is Christ Jesus who "became to us wisdom from God, righteousness and sanctification and redemption" (1 Cor 1:30 ESV). Therefore, in the presence of God, there is no other basis of boasting, and no other form of worth but Christ Jesus (1 Cor 1:31).

In 1 Corinthians 2:1-5, Paul draws upon his own personal experience to expound his point. Just as the Corinthians were lacking in notable qualities (1 Cor 1:26), Paul exposes his own weaknesses. He lacked eloquence and wisdom in his preaching (1 Cor 2:1). Instead of an impressively powerful presence, Paul exhibited weakness, fear, and trembling (1 Cor 2:3). He chose to focus only on Jesus Christ and his crucifixion (1 Cor 2:2). In short, his stature and style of preaching were contrary to the values of the Corinthians precisely so that *their faith* would be based not on "human wisdom, but on God's power" (1 Cor 2:5). Following parallel lines of argumentation, the two passages end with similar purpose statements:

> so that, as it is written, "Let the one who boasts, boast in the Lord." (1 Cor 1:31 ESV)

> so that your faith might not rest in the wisdom of men but in the power of God. (1 Cor 2:5 ESV)

The way he uses the verb *boasting* conveys the same dependence upon God implied in his use of the term *pistis*. This kind of boasting looks away from the self and to the Lord (1 Cor 1:31). Together, these two concepts reveal that human faith involves rejecting all earthly forms of worth. And yet, this does not leave the Corinthians empty-handed. Paul exhorts his readers to reorient their sense of worth in Christ alone. The correlation between boasting and faith in this passage reveals one essential element of true faith: what is true of Christ is true of oneself. In this way, faith redefines the self so that what is true of Christ becomes the ground of one's identity, hope, and value.

One more important underlying feature of Paul's view of faith is evident in 1 Corinthians 2:5 as he asserts the overarching purpose of this portion of the letter (1 Cor 1:18–2:5). Although entrenched within a society that prized eloquent and persuasive rhetoric, Paul eschewed such "lofty speech" in order that the Corinthians' faith might not rely on the wisdom of men but on the power of God (1 Cor 2:5). Here we see that the power of God draws out faith. Paul identifies this power in Christ himself (1 Cor 1:24)—it is represented in the cross and in Paul's preaching (1 Cor 1:17, 18; 2:2, 4-5). Thus, Christ is the clear focus of and power behind human faith.

Furthermore, as humans respond to the power of God in faith, they recognize their own inability to save themselves. Faith cannot be construed as a human work or self-contrived effort. In 1 Corinthians 1–2, Paul explains that God works through weakness, even the weakness of the cross. It is through that weakness that God's power is displayed (1 Cor 1:17). Faith then is the human response to that power of God and thus, faith is simultaneously self-negating and Christ affirming.

Relational faith in 1 Corinthians 15:1-2. The relational sense of faith is also evident in 1 Corinthians 15:1-2. Paul reminds the Corinthians that they had accepted and had actively responded to his preaching of the gospel message. As we observed above (1 Cor 2:5), salvation is predicated upon the divine act of God in Christ. However, Paul connects the Corinthians to the activity of God through his use of several "self-involving" verbs used to describe the Corinthians'

reception of the gospel:[3] "receiving," "standing," and "holding fast."
Furthermore, each verb seems to expound aspects of the final verb
(*pisteuō*) so that faith encompasses their meaning, as we shall see in
our analysis of the verbs below.

First, faith inevitably involves personally receiving the gospel. Receiving reflects active passivity. It is passive in that it requires the prior
action of another, the act of giving. Equally, receiving is active in ac-
cepting and appropriating the gift. Unique to the act of receiving the
divine gift is that the activity of the giver does not cease after the gift
has been received. The power of God that precedes and elicits reception continually empowers the receiver to appropriate the gift.
This is evident in 1 Thessalonians 2:13, where Paul speaks of receiving
the Word "which is *continually* at work in you believers" (author's
trans.). Just as the work of God is ongoing, so the receiver conveys a
sense of continuing and active dependence upon the giver. So, the
Corinthian reception of this gospel indicates, on one level, their
agreement with the propositions regarding the Christ-event—Christ
crucified, buried, and resurrected (1 Cor 15:3-4). Yet their reception
also indicates an active involvement with God who is at work in them.

The second self-involving verb that Paul employs portrays faith
metaphorically as "standing on" the truth of the gospel (1 Cor 15:1).
The gospel is symbolically presented as the ground upon which one
stands, depicting the idea of total dependence on Christ. In him, the
believer finds stability and security despite tribulation, temptation,
and affliction. Paul has already presented a similar metaphor earlier
in the letter when he contends that Jesus Christ alone is the *foundation* of the believers' existence (1 Cor 3:11). Again, at the close of the
chapter, Paul exhorts the Corinthians to "stand in faith" (1 Cor 16:13;
cf. Rom 11:20; 2 Cor 1:24). In 15:1, the perfect tense is used with the
sense of a past action with ongoing implications. In other words,
"standing in faith" is a present and persevering stability based on their
past decision to trust in the gospel. Through this metaphor, Paul

---

[3]This term, "self-involving," is borrowed from Anthony C. Thistleton, *The First Epistle to the Corinthians: A Commentary on the Greek Text*, NIGTC (Grand Rapids: Eerdmans, 2000), 720, 1184.

conveys faith as an ongoing confidence in Christ. The Christ-event—Jesus' death, burial, and resurrection—is the foundation upon which one lives through faith.

The third verb that Paul employs, "holding fast," also conveys faith as a continuing mode of existence through Paul's use of the present tense. Indeed, faith is not simply a decision made once in the past, but must be actively exercised. Paul seems to progress in his thought with each active verb that he employs, from the aorist (past) tense of the verb "to receive," conveying their past reception of the gospel, to the perfect tense of "to stand," which carries the force of their past reception into a present state of standing in dependence on the gospel, to concluding with a present tense verb expressing a contingency on their continuing to adhere to its truth.

In these important verses, we see that faith in the truth of the gospel of Jesus Christ is what forms the basis of the believers' new identity: it is that on which their past ("you received"), present ("you stand"), and future ("you are being saved") are based. In every way, faith is self-involving through active dependence on the Christ-event.

SUMMARY

In this chapter we have explored a broad survey of various understandings of faith in Greco-Roman philosophy to set the stage for a comparison between Plutarch and Paul's own understandings. Whereas the early Greek philosophical view of *pistis* often indicated an inferior intellectual state, Plutarch viewed *pistis* as being a firm foundation from which to view the world, even critiquing those who would demand proofs for faith. Paul makes an even stronger case for a rational basis of faith. In 1 Corinthians 15, he does not simply assert that the gospel is true, but provides evidence for the veracity of the faith through proofs and eyewitnesses.

Both Plutarch and Paul speak of *pistis* in the relational context of being faithful as well. Plutarch speaks widely of being trustworthy in a variety of relational and societal contexts. As to religious faith, for Plutarch being faithful entails imitating god to acquire his virtues. For

Paul, the relational components of faith run much deeper. Faith in God begins with first recognizing that Christ is the source of one's identity, hope, and worth. Faith looks away from the self and to Christ, conveying total dependence upon him alone. As a human posture, Paul demonstrates that it is not self-contrived but is elicited by, based upon, and directed toward Christ.

Paul's detailed explanation of the Corinthians' response to the Christ-event in 1 Corinthians 15:1-2 clarifies further the relational aspects of faith. As a confident, continuous standing upon Christ that holds fast through life while awaiting the culmination of our future salvation (1 Cor 15:19-58), faith is self-involving in Christ's very death and resurrection. Paul deliberately reminds the Corinthians of their existential response, urging that it continue to be reflected in ongoing acceptance and active dependence on the gospel of Jesus Christ. Ultimately, we see that for Paul, faith is the active mode of existence by which one connects oneself in a dependent relationship with God, identifying with the cross and participating in God's power through it.

For Further Reading

Primary Sources

Plutarch. *Lives*. [*Caesar* 22.] Translated by Bernadotte Perrin. LCL. London: Harvard University Press, 1919.

——. *Moralia*. Vol. 2. [*On Superstition*.] Translated by Frank Cole Babbitt. LCL. London: Harvard University Press, 1928.

——. *Moralia*. Vol. 7. [*On the Delays of Divine Vengeance*; *On Inoffensive Self-Praise*.] Translated by Philip H. De Lacy. LCL. London: Harvard University Press, 1959.

Secondary Sources

Bauer, Walter, William F. Arndt, F. Wilbur Gingrich, and Frederick W. Danker. *A Greek-English Lexicon of the New Testament and Other Early Christian Literature*. 3rd ed. Chicago: University of Chicago Press, 2000.

Bultmann, Rudolph. *Theology of the New Testament*. Translated by Kendrick Grobel. 2 vols. London: SCM Press, 1952.

Campbell, Douglas A. "Participation and Faith in Paul." In *"In Christ" in Paul: Explorations in Paul's Theology of Union and Participation*, edited by Michael

J. Thate, Kevin J. Vanhoozer, and Constantine R. Campbell, 37-60, WUNT 2/384. Tübingen: Mohr Siebeck, 2014.

Gorman, Michael J. *Becoming the Gospel: Paul, Participation, and Mission.* Grand Rapids: Eerdmans, 2015.

Kent, John Harvey. *Corinth: Results of Excavations Carried Out by the American School of Classical Studies at Athens, 8/3: The Inscriptions 1926–1950.* Princeton, NJ: ASCSA, 1966.

Kinneavy, James L. *Greek Rhetorical Origins of Christian Faith: An Inquiry.* Oxford: Oxford University Press, 1987.

Morgan, Teresa. *Roman Faith and Christian Faith:* Pistis *and* Fides *in the Early Roman Empire and Early Churches.* New York: Oxford University Press, 2015.

Pifer, Jeanette Hagen. *Faith as Participation: An Exegetical Study of Some Key Pauline Texts.* WUNT 2/486. Tübingen: Mohr Siebeck, 2019.

Thistleton, Anthony C. *The First Epistle to the Corinthians: A Commentary on the Greek Text.* NIGTC. Grand Rapids: Eerdmans, 2000.

Witherington, Ben, III. *Conflict & Community in Corinth: A Socio-rhetorical Commentary on 1 and 2 Corinthians.* Grand Rapids: Eerdmans, 1995.

DISCUSSION QUESTIONS

1. Which of the different definitions of faith in Greco-Roman philosophy do you see among those in your social and church settings?

2. What similarities and differences between Plutarch and Paul did you find most interesting?

3. Which of the various ways that Paul describes faith in 1 Corinthians were new to you? How have these aspects of faith helped to clarify or enhance your understanding of what it means to trust in the gospel or to trust in Christ?

4. What do you think of the idea of "self-involving" faith? Have you thought about how faith connects the believer to Christ's death and resurrection? How does that enhance or deepen your faith? How does this enhance your understanding of your identity in Christ?

7

WHEN IS A LETTER NOT A LETTER?

PAUL, CICERO, AND SENECA AS LETTER WRITERS

E. RANDOLPH RICHARDS

AROUND THE FIRST CENTURY, Greco-Roman letter writing was undergoing a gradual transformation from Cicero to Paul. Cicero commandeered the spontaneous, casual letter and used it for loftier purposes, bringing his rhetorical skills as an orator to the letter format. The political intrigues of Rome were navigated not just in the Roman courtroom but also on a papyrus sheet. That is to say, Cicero used what were supposedly private letters to navigate Roman politics, to negotiate conflict, to propagate his views, and to resolve issues.

Seneca likewise pushed everyday letters beyond what others were doing. He used letters to teach Stoic philosophy to his student Lucilius. The guise of a letter allowed the reader to put himself in Lucilius's place and to become Seneca's disciple too. In his letters, Seneca answered Lucilius's questions, which were questions any beginning student would ask. As the letters progressed and Lucilius grew in his understanding of Stoicism, Seneca put more advanced questions on Lucilius's lips. The reader, then, walked in Lucilius's shoes.

While this is a fascinating teaching strategy, something worth pointing out is that neither Cicero nor Seneca were using letters for their intended purpose. Most letters back then functioned like phone calls, emails, and texts today. Letters were written to tell loved ones about travel plans, business, or other routine matters. For example, in one letter, a young soldier wrote home to tell his mother where he was assigned by the Roman navy. So, what Cicero and Seneca were doing was not normal letter writing. Most ancients would have insisted their letters weren't letters!

Paul lived in the midst of this morphing tradition and availed himself of it. As we will see below, Paul wasn't your typical letter writer either. His letters are far too long and complex. Even Paul's opponents conceded that fact. They complained: "His letters are weighty and forceful" (2 Cor 10:10). Likely, by the term *weighty* they were ridiculing the length as well as the content. "Paul sends books, not letters," they were arguing. Before the Roman church ever unsealed his letter to read, they would have marveled at its size. Paul had sent them a book, not a letter!

Cicero and Seneca felt the freedom to reshape letter writing to their purposes. Paul did as well. Like Cicero, Paul used letters to navigate (church) politics, to negotiate conflict, to propagate his views, and to resolve issues. Like Seneca, Paul was teaching Christian philosophy: the gospel. Like Seneca, Paul wasn't informing; he was persuading. Both men intended their letters to make converts.

When Paul's letters are set alongside letters by Cicero and Seneca, we can better understand the letter writers and the letters they wrote. Now let's take a closer look, in which the superficial similarities in these letters will reveal the substantive differences among their authors.

LENGTH AND COST

Since we already mentioned in the introduction that letters by Paul, Cicero, and Seneca are much longer than the average letter, let's begin here. In more than 14,000 papyrus letters from Greco-Roman antiquity, the average length is about 87 words, ranging in length typically from 18 to 209 words. While Cicero was known for literary epistles and is considered to be one of the great letter writers of the Roman age, Seneca wrote even longer letters than he did. They are so exceptionally long that Seneca concedes: "I must not exceed the bounds of a letter, which ought not to fill the reader's left hand" (*Ep.* 45.13). This letter, *Epistle* 45, has 740 words, which would fill a standard *charta* (unit of sale for a papyrus roll). Seneca's two longest letters (*Ep.* 94 and 95) are considerably longer than his others: nearly 50 percent longer than his third longest letter and more than three times the size of his average letter. He describes one of the two longest letters as "a huge letter" (*Ep.* 95.3). Any fuller discussion, Seneca argues, would "be a book, instead of a letter" (*Ep.* 85.1). Seneca's five longest letters are *Epistles* 94 (4,201 words), 95 (4,105 words), 66 (3,006 words), 90 (2,971 words), and 88 (2,521 words); his five shortest are *Epistles* 62 (150 words), 38 (163 words), 112 (170 words), 34 (185 words), and 46 (193 words), with an average of 972 words.

Nonetheless, comparing Paul to Cicero and Seneca shows that Paul stands apart from *all* other known ancient letter writers.

Table 7.1. First table (length of letters)

	Shortest Letter	Longest Letter	Average Length
Cicero	22 words	2,530 words	295 words
Seneca	150 words	4,201 words	972 words
Paul	334 words	7,085 words	2,487 words

The length of Paul's letters, beyond merely blaming the verbosity of Paul, may be partially explained by noting that Paul likely held on to his letters, dispatching them when traveling season opened. Because Paul's letter carriers were required to traverse longer distances, the carrier may have often needed to await the opening of traveling season in late spring. This delay would allow Paul to write, edit, and append material over months, when Seneca would have dispatched the letter and sent another. Seneca presents himself as dispatching his letters frequently (*Ep.* 118.1). Frequent exchanges of letters, and thus a routine circulation of letter carriers, encouraged the swift ending of a letter. Cicero complained in a letter to Cassius that he had been rushed to finish so that the carrier could be on his way (*Fam.* 15.17.1-2). If we consider a letter of Paul commonly to have been composed over months, usually a winter while awaiting traveling season, then the length of Paul's letters is more understandable.

Paul's cost was aggravated by the excessive length of his letters.[1] To give you an idea, below are the costs (in today's American dollars) for the two longest and shortest letters of Paul and Seneca.

Table 7.2. Second table (cost of letters)

	Number of Characters	Total Cost in *Denars* for the Finished Letter	Cost Today (US Dollars)
Romans	34,232	20.68	$2,275
Philemon	1,562	0.93	$102
***Ep.* 94**	23,677	14.29	$1,572
***Ep.* 62**	829	0.48	$53

Due to his letters' high cost and the greater challenges of dispatching them, perhaps it was not mere rhetoric when Paul listed "concern for all the churches" as a great burden (2 Cor 11:28).

FREQUENCY

Obviously, a sender's (or recipient's) situation has a major impact on how often one writes. A sender's socioeconomic status, the distance from the sender (physically, socioeconomically, emotionally) also would impact how often one wrote. While Cicero wrote more frequently than Seneca and Paul, merely counting letters over a period of time obscures these factors. Nonetheless, for a better understanding, let's focus on the disparity in frequency between Seneca and Paul.

Seneca wrote at least 124 letters between the years AD 62 and 65. Whether or not these were actual missives, Seneca presents himself as writing at this frequency, suggesting it was not an unreasonable scenario. If we accept a generous Pauline collection and then add the two so-called lost letters to Corinth (cf. 1 Cor 5:9; 2 Cor 7:8), we can credit Paul with up to fifteen letters over a fifteen-year period. Thus, Seneca wrote (or at least presented himself as writing) about forty letters a year, while Paul wrote about one a year. When we restrict the comparison

---

[1]For literary works, copyists used an average hexameter line of sixteen syllables for a total of about 36 characters per line. This line was called a *stichos*. Copyists charged by the number of *stichoi*; books were priced in this way. Private letters appear to have conformed to this standard. Published copies of Seneca's collection certainly would have.

to Paul's time under Roman confinement, we can double Paul's frequency, but then only about two letters a year. At the very least, we can safely say Seneca was a far more frequent letter writer than Paul.

The contrast between Seneca (and Cicero) and Paul is great enough to seem significant. How might we explain it? Likely, leisure and wealth account for Seneca's frequency. If his letters were ever missives, then we should also note he lived near Lucilius. This allowed letter carriers to travel even outside of traditional traveling season. The seasonal limits for land and sea travel did not apply to local travel on the lower Italian peninsula. Seneca noted that sea travel would delay a letter (*Ep.* 71.1). Similarly, Cicero exchanged frequent letters across a short geographical distance.

If (as seems likely) close geographical proximity allowed a faster exchange of correspondence, then it may be worth comparing the one instance where Paul corresponded with a congregation nearby: letters to Corinth while living in Ephesus. Scholars commonly assert Paul wrote at least four letters within two years. While this is still far less frequent than Cicero and Seneca, it is more frequent than was Paul's custom. Paul's busyness, frequent travels, greater distances, and increased expense probably account for Paul writing fewer letters.

Private or Public Letters?

In the early twentieth century when archaeologists began uncovering papyrus letters in the sands of Egypt, it was quickly noticed how dissimilar these papyrus letters were from the letters of Cicero, Seneca, and other Roman aristocrats and yet how similar the vocabulary of these papyri was to Paul's letters. Adolf Deissmann drew a strong distinction between these highly occasioned papyrus *letters* and the artificial, artistic literary *epistles*.[2]

Typical papyrus letters were natural, daily, situational letters, intended to be read by the recipient only. Literary epistles, although

---

[2]See Adolf Deissmann, *Light from the Ancient Near East: The New Testament Illustrated by Recently Discovered Texts of the Graeco-Roman World*, trans. L. R. M. Strachan (London: Hodder & Stoughton, 1912), 290-301; see also E. Randolph Richards, *Paul and First Century Letter Writing: Secretaries, Composition and Collection* (Downers Grove, IL: InterVarsity Press, 2004), 122-27.

addressed to an individual, usually a friend or patron, were actually written for anyone willing and able to read them, with the true purpose of persuading the general public to a particular viewpoint. Since Paul used the same "street language" that Deissmann found in the papyrus letters, Paul was quickly reclassified with them. Paul's letters, Deissmann argued, must be read as artless, spontaneous letters, forged in the crucible of ministry, dashed off in the flurry of life, and certainly never intended to be read by others. Thus, Paul should not be compared at all to someone like Cicero or Seneca.

Deissmann's distinction flourished for a while but eventually fell out of vogue as too artificial. When not overstated, however, his categories can be useful. We should view ancient letters, though, not as two options but rather as on a spectrum from very public, long, artificial epistles to highly occasioned, short, private letters. Seneca would be a fine, if not the finest, example of the epistle endpoint of the spectrum. The papyri from the Egyptian desert provide bounteous examples of the letter endpoint. Paul however remains somewhere in the middle, difficult to classify, having qualities of both epistle and letter.

Figure 2. Letter-epistle spectrum

Can we at least describe Paul's letters as private and Seneca's as public? No. While Seneca's letters pose as very personal correspondence, scholars generally agree the letters were intended for a broad if not public audience. Ironically, Paul's letters present themselves as rather public. They are sometimes from a team (Gal; 1 and 2 Thess), often with a co-sender (1 and 2 Cor; Phil; Col; Philem), and are usually addressed to a community. Yet Paul's letters certainly read as more personal than those of Seneca. We cannot simplistically label one writer as composing public letters and the other private ones. Paul's letters don't fit neatly into a category. His are letters that are not really letters, at least not when compared to the papyrus letters.

FORMAL OR CASUAL

First-century Mediterranean letters were remarkably consistent in format, whether written in Greek (Paul) or Latin (Cicero and Seneca).[3] What's significant is not so much the difference in language as much as the difference in *quality* of language. Take Paul and Seneca's style for example. While Paul's Greek is routinely characterized as unpolished, Seneca's letters *claim* a casual style. For example, in *Epistle 85*, Seneca writes: "I prefer that my letters should be just what my conversation would be if you and I were sitting in one another's company" (*Ep.* 85.1). Elsewhere Seneca even places such an accusation on the lips of Lucilius: "You complain that you receive from me letters which are rather carelessly written" (*Ep.* 75.1).

In contrast to Paul's letters, however, an analysis of Seneca's letters refutes Seneca's claims. The Stoic's letters are carefully crafted, balancing thought to style, judiciously selecting the most effective words. Seneca was a master rhetorician. Whenever he seems careless in his writing, it is actually to make a point. Whereas Seneca's claims to carelessness are a ruse and his seeming casualness is artificial, Paul actually has grammatical slips in his letters that give his letters a genuine *koine* (everyday) quality, reflecting the language of the street.

The differences in their letters mirror somewhat the differences in the men. Paul was a member of a conquered people within the empire, while Cicero and Seneca were members of the ruling elite. Paul would have been viewed/received quite differently, even if they had shared similar economic or educational status, which they certainly did not. A vast economic chasm existed between Paul and them. They lived in different worlds. For instance, Seneca mentioned having the luxury to turn down delicacies such as oysters and mushrooms, because

---

[3]However, while Paul frequently uses phrases common in letter writing (epistolary formulae), Seneca rarely does. Moreover, ancient letters commonly mention prayers to the gods. But Paul prays at more length and for very different things than those prayers (e.g., 2 Cor 13:7, 9; Eph 1:18; 3:14). Seneca rarely mentions prayer at all.

"they are not really food, but are relishes to bully the sated stomach into further eating" (*Ep.* 108.15). Paul, in contrast, knew what it was to have need and occasionally experience genuine hunger (Phil 4:12; 2 Cor 6:5). Their vast socioeconomic differences would have ensured that the Roman philosopher would not have noticed the Jew, Paul, even if he had walked past the other on the street.

CONCLUSION

As we have seen, comparing Paul's letters with those of Cicero and Seneca reveals that the apostle's works are exceptionally longer than even the long letters of his time (e.g., those from Cicero and Seneca). Consequently, Paul's were far more costly. Although he wrote longer letters, he did not write them as often as Cicero or Seneca. In addition to the increased expense, this likely reflected Paul's busy schedule and ministry trips as well as the greater distances between him and his audience. Further, while Seneca's letters purport to be personal, they are really public, and Paul's letters present themselves as more public yet seem deeply personal. Seneca was supposedly writing to a friend, but his letters show no real marks of friendship, community, or genuine personal concern, but Paul's letters were written to communities, sometimes communities scattered across a city or even a province, with whom he had a deep personal connection.

Although Paul, Cicero, and Seneca are not literary cousins, none of the three is like the typical letter writer. Therefore, when is a letter *not* a letter? When Paul, Cicero, or Seneca is writing. For these men, letters were tools to be reshaped in the hands of a master, bending the letter to their purposes. Since the men had different purposes, we should not be surprised that their letters ended up different from typical letters but also different from each other. All three wanted to flood the world with their ideas. The major difference is that Paul claimed his gospel came from God (1 Thess 2:13).

FOR FURTHER READING

Deissmann, Adolf. *Light from the Ancient Near East: The New Testament Illustrated by Recently Discovered Texts of the Graeco-Roman World.* Translated by Lionel R. M. Strachan. London: Hodder & Stoughton, 1912. Reprint, Grand Rapids: Baker, 1978.

Klauck, Hans-Josef. *Ancient Letters and the New Testament: A Guide to Context and Exegesis.* Waco, TX: Baylor University Press, 2006.

Richards, E. Randolph. *Paul and First-Century Letter Writing: Secretaries, Composition and Collection.* Downers Grove, IL: InterVarsity Press, 2004.

Discussion Questions

1. Paul listed "concern for all the churches" (2 Cor 11:28) as one of the burdens he endured. Considering the unusual length of his letters and the time and expense he spent, how should we evaluate the popular movement today among many Christian leaders to dismiss or discount the church, often as too much bother?

2. We saw there was a popular trend among the intellectuals of Paul's day to use letters—the common means of everyday communication—for loftier purposes. Paul adopted this practice. Today, we have different methods of communication. How might Paul's willingness to adopt and adapt new methods inspire Christian leaders today? Give some specific examples.

3. For Paul, ministry was always personal. He described himself in one breath as both a father (1 Thess 2:11) and a nursing mother (1 Thess 2:7) to the Thessalonians. They were his children. For Paul, ministry was never just a job. His letters *showed* he hurt for them, worried over them, and cared deeply for them. Obviously, Christian leaders should love those under their care, but what can we learn from how Paul communicated to his congregants?

4. Both Seneca and Paul considered their recipient(s) to be their handiwork (*Ep.* 34.1; 2 Cor 3:1-3), with whom they were of one mind (*Ep.* 35.2), but Paul mentioned it more often and in fewer letters and was more concerned that his disciples were of one mind with each other (Rom 15:6; 1 Cor 1:10; 2 Cor 13:11; Phil 2:2). Why do you think this is the case?

8

FIGHTING THE GOOD FIGHT

THE GOOD LIFE IN PAUL AND THE GIANTS OF PHILOSOPHY

NIJAY K. GUPTA

As FAR AS WE KNOW, the apostle Paul never fought in a physical battle as a soldier. Yet it is clear he was fond of using military metaphors in his letters. In 2 Corinthians, for example, he talks about the servants of God being ready with "weapons of righteousness" for each hand (2 Cor 6:7). Sometimes his martial imagery is overt, as with the above example. Other times it is less explicit, but detectable nonetheless. For instance, Paul encourages his converts to "stand firm" in the Lord, a military phrase indicating the expectations placed on soldiers, that is, "the taking of a position vis-a-vis that of an adversary."[1] Of course, Paul used a wide variety of metaphors in his letters: sacrifice, athletics, body and head, sowing and reaping, and so on. But remarkably, martial imagery appears in almost all of Paul's letters with interest in guiding the Christian life.

In a moment, we will consider several reasons why Paul may have used such language, and to what end, but initially we can simply assume that military imagery would have come to mind because it was everywhere in the Roman world. As Warren Carter explains, "It is not surprising that people living in a context of military power and subordinated to its power should absorb this military ethos and

---

[1]Timothy Geoffrion, *The Rhetorical Purpose and the Political and Military Character of Philippians* (Lewiston, NY: Mellen Biblical Press, 1993), 55.

language whether they want to or not."[2] Indeed, in the Greco-Roman world there was a long tradition of using such word pictures to talk about life in general. As far back as the sixth century BC, we find philosophers (like Pythagoras) comparing the path to the good life to that of the noble soldier.[3] As Laurie Brink explains,

> The rigors of military life became a metaphor for the austere lifestyle of the philosopher and the pursuit of virtue. Long after the battle, the successful general embodied a model for rhetoricians in their creation of *encomia*, (speeches or writings that praise someone or something). In the hands of playwrights and poets, the blood of battle became the source of inspiration for comic triumphs and dramatic tragedies.[4]

Paul, then, would have been utilizing a popular cultural tradition of teaching virtue and wisdom via the "good soldier" theme. When we observe Paul's military metaphors closely, we find numerous parallels between his usage and aims and those of Greek and Roman philosophers of his day. That is not to say Paul himself intentionally studied the works of philosophers to imitate their styles of discourse. After all, he never mentions any philosophers by name in his writings, nor does he appear to quote them explicitly. But since Paul seems to have been a "cultured" person, he probably had a general familiarity with popular philosophers and their main works or ideas. (We might compare this to the way we come to learn about plots of movies we haven't seen based on social media chatter and "water cooler" talk.) When we compare Paul's moral teaching with that of the ancient philosophers, it is rather striking to observe the similarities. In this chapter, we will compare Paul and the philosophers on four subjects: life is a battle, the good soldier's courage, the good soldier's obedience and cooperation, and the good soldier's self-discipline.

---

[2]Warren Carter, *The Roman Empire and the New Testament* (Nashville: Abingdon, 2010), 24.
[3]See Geoffrion, *Rhetorical Purpose*, 38.
[4]Laurie Brink, *Soldiers in Luke-Acts*, WUNT 2/362 (Tübingen: Mohr Siebeck, 2014), 1.

Life Is a Battle

The best place to start demonstrating why Paul and the philosophers used martial imagery is with the prevalent notion that "life is a battle." If life were easy or simple, there would presumably be no need for such language, and, frankly, there would probably be no need for moral writings at all. Both Paul and (most of) the ancient philosophers, however, firmly believed that moral instruction was necessary because hardships were inevitable and mortals remain immature and weak without *paideia*—instruction in wisdom and maturity. The image of the "good soldier," then, would properly awaken people to these challenges and opportunities and inspire them to be ready for a difficult but potentially rewarding path forward. In Galatians, Paul explains that the world is plagued by a continuous battle between flesh and spirit: "They are in conflict with each other" (Gal 5:17). The same concept is probably present when Paul warns the Thessalonians to be "awake" and "sober" (1 Thess 5:6) the way soldiers stand watch at night for fear the enemy might attack them under the cloak of darkness and the vulnerability of fatigue. The Greek Stoic Epictetus presents this statement in this way:

> Don't you know life is like a military campaign? One must serve on watch, another in reconnaissance, another on the front line. . . . So it is for us—each person's life is a kind of battle, and a long and varied one too. You must keep watch like a soldier and do everything commanded. . . . You have been stationed in a key post, not some lowly place, and not for a short time but for life. (*Disc.* 3.24.31-36)

The Roman Stoic Seneca similarly wrote, "to live is to engage in military conflict" (*Ep.* 96.5). Part of the reason why Seneca holds up the "good soldier" for admiration is how these men live life with the utmost sobriety. In a letter to Lucilius, Seneca praises the attitude of the Roman soldier. Sometimes, the soldier is travelling merrily and enjoying the journey, but at a moment's notice he springs into action, aware of a nearby threat; "necessity makes him throw away everything which he picked up in moments of peace and leisure" (49.6). What Seneca refers to here is the soldier's indifference toward worldly pleasures that pass away and his need to invest in things that will carry on past his demise. For "Death," writes Seneca, "is on my trail, and life is fleeting away" (49.9).

If life is a battle, who or what is the enemy? This is where we see a divergence between Paul and the ancient moral philosophers. As we have already mentioned, Paul conveyed to his converts the idea that "flesh" and "spirit" are in constant and continuous conflict, one trying to conquer the other. The believer is forced to side with one of these, not just once, but in each moment (Rom 8:4-9, 13; Gal 5:16-17; cf. Phil 3:3). Perhaps most distinctively, Paul saw the primal "enemies" as "sin" and "death." Now, one might expect a Jew like Paul to focus on the wiles of Satan and the power of evil—and Paul does not neglect these foes (Rom 12:21; 16:20; 2 Cor 2:11; 11:14; 12:7; 1 Thess 2:18). But he gives more attention to the twin powers of sin and death. Paul talks about sin as if it is a monster that infiltrated the earth, taking advantage of the weak state of humanity when Adam sinned (Rom 5:12). So too death followed along, and both have wreaked cataclysmic havoc ever since (Rom 5:12). Thus, Paul could attest that "death reigned from the time of Adam to the time of Moses" (Rom 5:14), and "sin reigned in death" (Rom 5:21). Mortals, then, are in the pitiable situation of being slaves of sin. But Paul believed that through the redemptive power of the gospel of Jesus Christ, believers could be freed from sin and death and become "slaves of righteousness" (Rom 6:16-18; cf. 1 Cor 15:56-57). Paul did not think in terms of "virtue" and "vice" per se, but he believed that some values and behaviors are in keeping with the true kingdom of God, while others demonstrate languishing in the flesh.

For many of the ancient philosophers, like Socrates, the primary concern was the war against passions.[5] Seneca, as a Stoic, believed that one had to face the realities of "fate" and inevitable hardships, and ultimately one was called to resist temptation and control human desires (see *Ep.* 87.41; 95.5). Roman orator Cicero offers a helpful snapshot

---

[5]See *Xen., Mem.* 1.2.24; as cited in C. S. Keener, *The Mind of the Spirit: Paul's Approach to Transformed Thinking* (Grand Rapids: Baker Academic, 2016), 110n407.

of his philosophical attitude toward life: "That person . . . whose mind is quiet through consistency and self-control, who finds contentment in himself, and neither breaks down in adversity nor crumbles in fright, nor burns with any thirsty need nor dissolves into wild and futile excitement, that person is the wise one we are seeking, and that person is happy" (*Tusculan Disputations* 4.37).[6] The Jewish philosopher Philo of Alexandria captures well the philosopher's ideal; Philo compared the Old Testament focus on "rest" in the "land" to the philosopher's pursuit of pure virtue. Just as Israel had to undertake an arduous and perilous journey to Canaan, so the wise man must face much hardship in pursuit of virtue, so much so that the path requires battle with the enemies of vice and passion (*Somn.* 174).

THE GOOD SOLDIER'S COURAGE

In the minds of Greeks and Romans, the most prominent trait of the good soldier was *virtus*, which means "manliness" or "courage." Roman playwright Plautus (254–184 BC) demonstrates the cultural prominence of this value in the words of a wife:

> I want my man to be cried as a victor of war: that's enough for me. *Virtus* is the greatest prize; *virtus* comes before everything, that's certain. . . . *Virtus* has everything in it: who has *virtus* has everything good. (*Amph.* 6.48-54)[7]

If someone wanted to get a sense for how Romans understood this virtue of courage, one might read over Plutarch's *Sayings of Spartans*, a kind of *Reader's Digest* of manly one-liners and pithy anecdotes. One such logion is attributed to Agesilaus: "a general ought to be possessed of boldness towards the enemy and kindness towards men under him" (213C). In Seneca's *On Providence*, he reasons that hardships are not only survivable, but even beneficial, because true strength comes from finding courage to endure and overcome difficulties. Seneca writes, "I judge you unfortunate because you have

---

[6]See Nancy Sherman, *Stoic Warriors* (Oxford: Oxford University Press, 2007), xiv.
[7]As cited in J. E. Lendon, *Soldiers and Ghosts: A History of Battle in Classical Antiquity* (New Haven, CT: Yale University Press, 2005), 176.

never been unfortunate. You have passed through life without an antagonist; no one will know what you can do—not even yourself" (4.3). He goes on: "Great men, I say, rejoice oft-times in adversity, as do brave soldiers in warfare. . . . True worth is eager for danger and thinks rather of its goal than of what it may have to suffer, since even what it will have to suffer is a part of its glory" (4.4). I wonder if Paul would not offer nods of agreement to Seneca's climactic statement, "Disaster is virtue's opportunity" (4.6).

As observed above, courage is about the spurning of fear and timidity, but ultimately the good soldier ought to show such sterling bravery that he has no hesitation about facing death itself. Seneca muses on this subject at length in his discourse *Despising Shame* (*Ep.* 24). He endeavors to teach Lucilius that the great heroes of history dared to defy the specter of death. He offers the example of a certain general Scipio. Seeing his ship captured by enemies, Scipio plunged his sword into his own body. When his soldiers asked about the whereabouts of the commander, Scipio replied, "All is well with the commander" (24.9). Seneca adds, "It was a great deed to conquer Carthage, but a greater deed to conquer death" (24.10).

Jewish historian Josephus extols the valor of a Roman centurion named Julianus. In a certain battle, with the Romans all but beaten, Julianus dared to rush the enemy all on his own. He fought so bravely and powerfully that he pushed back the opposition and scared them into retreat "regarding such strength and courage as superhuman" (*J.W.* 6.82, LCL). Consequently, Josephus explains that this feat of *virtus* made Julianus known to the emperor himself, and his name brought terror to enemies far and wide (6.83).

When we compare this to the apostle Paul, we get the sense that he too respected the virtue of courage, and even framed the Christian struggle against evil as akin to that of the intrepid soldier. To give one obvious example, to the Corinthians Paul writes, "Keep alert, stand firm in your faith, *be courageous*, be strong" (1 Cor 16:13 NRSV, emphasis added). Paul exhorted the Corinthians to be brave because many early believers faced terrible persecution and temptations toward giving in to all manner of cultural vices. He could invoke the image of the good soldier to reframe life as a battle to be won; that way they could see that this opposition served a purpose and their allegiance to Jesus Christ was a sign of *virtus*—culturally speaking, the virtue of virtues.

Perhaps the most vivid Pauline portrayal of the good soldier's courage is found in his letter to the Philippians, written when Paul was enchained in prison and the believers in Philippi were suffering severe persecution. In order to re-imagine how the Philippians thought about their (and his) situation, he portrayed their circumstances as one of a suppressed army in need of a pep talk. In the first chapter, Paul refers to their "struggle," using the Greek word *agōn*, which means "conflict" and conjures up images of battle (Phil 1:30). In chapter 2, he calls their emissary (Epaphroditus) a "fellow soldier" (Phil 2:25) and commends him for his bravery, "risking his life" to bring aid to Paul (Phil 2:30). Paul's sending back of Epaphroditus to Philippi was like an honorable discharge, and Paul wanted to ensure he received a hero's welcome on return.

Paul also commends several people in his letters whom he calls "fellow prisoners," certain believers who apparently spent time in chains with Paul (Rom 16:7; Philem 23; Col 4:10). English translations have trouble conveying the idea that, in these particular instances, Paul uses the specific language of (fellow) prisoners *of war*.[8] All of this helps to communicate how serious of a mission the gospel is, and that the church is like an army called to dauntless faith as believers seek to overcome evil for the sake of salvation. For those who face hardship and opposition, they ought to imagine themselves as spiritual soldiers in need of courage and strength to win the battle for God's kingdom in Jesus Christ.

The Good Soldier's Obedience and Cooperation

The primary and most dominant virtue of the good soldier is *virtus* (courage), as explained above, and this tends to be the focal point of the

---

[8]In these instances, Paul uses the Greek word *synaichmalōtos*, which means "prisoner of war," rather than the more common word *desmios*, which means "chained person"; see Murray J. Harris, *Slave of Christ* (Downers Grove, IL: InterVarsity Press, 1999), 117.

good soldier theme, but it is worth mentioning here the cultural appreciation for the good soldier's virtue of obedience or compliance. It was well-known in Paul's time that soldiers swore exclusive allegiance to the emperor. So, Epictetus could use this concept to inspire ultimate respect for God: "you have to maintain the character of a soldier, and do each separate act at the bidding of the General, if possible divining what He wishes" (*Diatr.* 3.24.34-35). Seneca offers a similar perspective, mentioning the soldier's devotion to the imperial image on the battalion flag and the shame associated with the basest of military vices, desertion (*Ep.* 95.35). In his *On Clemency*, Seneca expands on this notion. For the sake of the honor of the sovereign, Roman troops would gladly "expose their breasts to wounds" because the king is "the bond which fastens the commonwealth together" (*Clem.* 4). The same idea seems to be at work in Paul when he exhorts the Philippians to stand firm "in the Lord" (Phil 4:1). When believers engage in battle, they destroy strongholds and opposing arguments against the knowledge of God that leads to one's allegiance and obedience to Christ (2 Cor 10:5).

The common assumption here is that the good soldier is not self-focused; he sees himself as a servant of the emperor and as a piece of a whole (army unit). The Cynic Antisthenes lauds the selfless character of the hero Odysseus who risked his own life to save his associates.[9] Josephus esteems the unity and efficiency of the Roman army. He also praises their warfare success, attributing it not to luck or happenstance, but to their firm commitment and rigorous training. According to Josephus, they practice and train constantly, which not only helps them to be prepared, but also increases their endurance (*J. W.* 3.71-73). He goes so far as to say that one could call their training "unbloody battles" but their actual battles "bloody exercises" (3.75). To the point of our discussion of compliance and unity, Josephus observes how their lifestyle is marked by "good order and security" (3.85).[10] They eat in unison and their chores are perfectly

---

[9]See R. Collins, *The Power of Images in Paul* (Collegeville, MN: Liturgical Press, 2008), 170-71.
[10]"Security" here seems to mean caution and precision.

synchronized (3.86). When they engage in combat, "the whole army is but one body" (3.104).

> This perfect discipline makes the army an ornament of peace-time and in war welds the whole into a single body; so compact are their ranks, so alert their movements in wheeling to right or left, so quick their ears for orders, their eyes for signals, their hands to act upon them. Prompt as they consequently ever are in action, none are slower than they to succumb to suffering, and never have they been known in any predicament to be beaten by numbers, by ruse, by difficulty of ground, or even by fortune; for they have more assurance of victory than of fortune. (3.105-6 LCL)

Again, according to Josephus they embody a selfless unity that allows them to multiply their strengths and success. One wonders if Paul had just such an image in mind when he called the Philippians to unity in life and mission. At the end of Philippians 1, Paul enjoins them to live as good citizens worthy of the gospel of Christ, which can be demonstrated in their "standing firm in one spirit, striving side by side with one mind for the faith of the gospel" (Phil 1:27 NRSV). Only a few verses later, he states one of his primary hopes for their community: "be[ing] of the same mind, having the same love, being in full accord and of one mind" (Phil 2:2 NRSV). In chapter 4, Paul calls out Euodia and Syntyche who have been arguing. They ought to be "of the same mind in the Lord" (Phil 4:2). Despite this admonishment, he commends them as women who have "struggled beside me in the work of the gospel" (Phil 4:3). In Philippi—a city full of Roman war veterans and many battle stories passed around over the years—it would be no surprise that Paul would employ military language to talk about unity and obedience.

THE GOOD SOLDIER'S SELF-DISCIPLINE

The last theme we will briefly mention is closely related to the others—the good soldier's self-discipline and moderation. The life of a soldier was supposed to be austere and strict. Although soldiers received alcohol as part of their rations, they were prohibited from getting drunk. They were also not allowed to marry. That did not prevent them from having sex, but it did signal that their "commitments" were strictly to their duties. The emperor called them to "restraint and self-control."[11] Seneca could point to soldiers when he waxed on about the difference between *virtus* and *voluptas* (pleasure).

> *Virtus* you will find in the temple, in the forum, in the senate house, defending the city's walls, dusty and suntanned, with rough hands; pleasure you will find most often lurking and seeking shade around the baths and sweating rooms, and places that fear the magistrates, soft, effete, reeking of wine and perfume, pallid or else painted and made up like a corpse. (*Beat.* 7.4)

One might compare this to Paul's appeal in Romans 13:12-14, where he calls the Roman believers to don the "armor of light" (Rom 13:12). This involves discarding "works of darkness," choosing to respect propriety and to reject revelry, drunkenness, debauchery, and dissension (Rom 13:13). Wearing the Lord Jesus Christ ought to entail resistance to the flesh and its passions (Rom 13:14).

CONCLUSION

These brief comparisons between Paul and the philosophers on the "good soldier" and the "good life" demonstrate remarkable conceptual and rhetorical overlap. To the degree that Paul knew how powerful such cultural images and ideals could be, he was able to utilize them to talk about faith in Jesus Christ and Christian vigilance in view of the attacks by sin and death. Of course, despite his frequent use of war language, Paul was deeply committed to peace and mercy. In the lists of hardships we find in his letters, he notes with pride his endurance of suffering and mockery (e.g., 2 Cor 11:23-27). There is no mention of retaliation (for honor or safety) or revenge. Nevertheless, he followed a long biblical tradition, present in Greco-Roman culture as well, of perceiving life as a battle. For Paul, though, the end was not the glory of Rome or *Elysium*, but glory to God, because of whom believers are "more than conquerors" over sin and evil through the gospel and love of Jesus Christ (Rom 8:37).

---

[11]Caesar BG VII 52.1.

For Further Reading

Primary Sources
Josephus. *The Jewish War*. Translated by H. St. J. Thackeray. LCL. London: Harvard University Press, 1927–1928.

Plautus. *The Comedies*. Vol. 1. Edited by David R. Slavitt and Palmer Bovie. Baltimore: Johns Hopkins University Press, 1995.

Plutarch. *Moralia*. Vol. 3. Translated by Frank Cole Babbitt. LCL. London: Harvard University Press, 1931.

Seneca. *Moral Essays*. Translated by John W. Basore. LCL. London: Harvard University Press, 2003.

Secondary Sources
Collins, R. *The Power of Images in Paul*. Collegeville, MN: Liturgical Press, 2008.

Geoffrion, Timothy. *The Rhetorical Purpose and the Political and Military Character of Philippians*. Lewiston, NY: Mellen Biblical Press, 1993.

Krentz, Edgar. "Military Language and Metaphors in Philippians." In *Origins and Method: Towards a New Understanding of Judaism and Christianity*, edited by Bradley H. McLean, 105-27, JSNTSup 86. Sheffield: Sheffield Academic Press, 1993.

Lendon, J. E. *Soldiers and Ghosts: A History of Battle in Classical Antiquity*. New Haven, CT: Yale University Press, 2005.

Sherman, Nancy. *Stoic Warriors*. Oxford: Oxford University Press, 2007.

Wansink, C. S. *Chained in Christ: The Experience and Rhetoric of Paul's Imprisonments*. JSNTSup 130. Sheffield: Sheffield Academic Press, 1996.

Discussion Questions

1. Why did Paul talk about the Christian life using metaphorical language of warfare?

2. How is Paul's martial language similar to the philosophers of his time? How is it different?

3. How do you think his first-century readers would have received this warfare language?

4. How do you reconcile Paul's violent metaphors with his commitment to "peace"?

9

STRINGS ATTACHED

PAUL AND SENECA ON THE MODERN MYTH OF THE PURE GIFT[1]

DAVID E. BRIONES

WHY IS IT THAT WE RESPECT PEOPLE who give anonymous checks to charities? Why do we admire those who secretly give money to a struggling couple? Why do we esteem those who give gifts and insist that there are "no strings attached," no obligation to give a return gift, no expectation to reciprocate? Why do we honor them as *the* model of selfless virtue? It's because we believe that their generosity is patterned after *the* "purest" model of gift giving.

"PURE" GIFT GIVING?

Have you ever heard someone say something like, "The purest kind of giving is the way God gives—without strings attached"? God, they would argue, gives to us without seeking anything in return. God's giving is "pure"; there is no self-interest, no obligation, no expectation of a return gift. Underlying this "pure" perspective on God's giving is a sharp distinction between two economies: the *market* economy and the *gift* economy. Givers within the market economy are self-interested. They obligate others and demand reciprocity. But givers within the gift economy do the opposite. They give spontaneously, voluntarily, unconditionally, and freely, with "no strings attached." The market economy is "impure," while the gift economy is entirely

---

[1] I am indebted to my Doktorvater, John M. G. Barclay, for the title of this chapter and for many of the thoughts contained within.

"pure." Why? Again, because it is said to imitate *the* divine model of gift giving set by the "purest" being in the universe, God himself.

But what if I told you that giving with no strings attached is a recent phenomenon? What if you discovered that no one thought this way in the ancient world? What if you learned that this way of thinking about gift giving had more in common with post-Enlightenment philosophy (especially Immanuel Kant) than biblical Christianity? More straightforward, what if I told you that the notion of the "pure" gift is a modern myth? Would you believe me?

Does not the sharp distinction between the *market* economy and *gift* economy already begin to plant seeds of doubt in your mind? Are these really two distinct spheres of life without any point of contact whatsoever? Think about Christmas Day. Let's assume, for the sake of argument, that Christmas gifts wrapped in the paper of self-interest and obligation—those dirty features of giving in the market economy—makes them "impure." Those so-called gifts would carry the stench of the marketplace rather than the fresh scent of Christmas morning, right?

"Of course," you say. Giving and receiving on Christmas takes place in the sphere of relationship, where gifts tangibly express love and concern among close friends and family members. This sphere is very much unlike the exploitative sphere of the marketplace. Little to no relationship exists there. I can easily buy an item from a store without any regard for the employee behind the register. I only have my interests and my needs in view. It seems as if there can be no point of contact between these two distinct economies or spheres.

Or is there? Do we really think that if there is any self-interest, obligation, or reciprocity in our giving, then our gifts are no longer gifts? That they are now impure commodities? If that were the case, would not all our gifts be considered impure commodities? Who has ever given a gift on Christmas morning without expecting a gift in return? What parent, after giving a gift to their child, doesn't gladly receive joy in return? That sounds a lot like self-interest. Who has ever received a gift from someone without feeling compelled to give a counter-gift lest you seem ungrateful? That sounds a lot like obligation and reciprocity.

These hidden feelings and subtle expectations reveal a sort of double-mindedness about gift giving. Ideally, we praise the disinterested, unconditional gift. But in reality we acknowledge the inescapable truth that our giving exhibits the very "impure" features we abhor: self-interest, obligation, and reciprocity. This may lead us to the conclusion drawn by the French philosopher Jacques Derrida, who declared that a "pure" gift is utterly impossible. He argued that the only possible "pure" gift a person can give is the gift of death, since it's impossible for a dead person to expect anything in return!

In what follows, I will seek to show that the notion of the "pure" gift is indeed a modern myth. I will do so by considering the ancient perspectives of two very different thinkers, Paul and Seneca. Although worlds apart philosophically and theologically, they have much in common on this point.

SENECA ON THE MODERN MYTH OF THE PURE GIFT[2]

Setting his ancient context. Seneca wrote the major work on gift giving in the first-century world. It is entitled *On Benefits*. Hailed as a masterpiece by many classicists, this work seeks to oil the machinery of gift giving in ancient Roman society. Seneca is convinced that giving, receiving, and returning benefits "constitutes the chief bond of human society" (*Ben.* 1.4.2), and for that reason, he goes to great lengths to preserve this vital practice. But he encounters many problems along the way.

To begin with, ancient society is wicked: "wicked we are, wicked we have been, and, I regret to add, always shall be" (1.10.3). But above all the immorality in society, such as "tyrants, thieves, adulterers, robbers, sacrilegious men, and traitors," the most heinous vice, and perhaps the root of all these other vices, is ingratitude (1.10.4). If left unchecked, the wickedness of ingratitude in society will destroy the

---

[2]For an expansion of the ideas in this section, please see my *Paul's Financial Policy: A Socio-Theological Approach*, LNTS 494 (London: Bloomsbury, 2013), 41-57.

system of giving and receiving. He therefore takes philosophical aim at ungrateful givers and receivers, but he especially criticizes givers.

Of course, givers didn't think they were the ones to blame. They were pointing the finger at their ungrateful recipients. But Seneca knows better. A big part of the problem is that givers do not employ reason and discernment in their giving. That is, they do "not pick out those who are worthy of receiving their gifts" (1.1.2; cf. 3.11.1). Not doing so will inevitably produce ungrateful recipients, for "if we did not select the one to whom we were giving, *the fault is our own*" (4.10.3; my italics).

Seneca also criticizes the manner of their giving. Some benefactors delay their gifts (2.6.1-2). Others immediately give gifts, but the way they do so makes it seem as if the recipients were robbing them (2.1.2). Still others would not stop mentioning how beneficent they have been. Seneca paints an amusing picture of a man who, after being freed from the hand of Caesar by a benefactor, cries out, "Give me back to Caesar!" because this liberated person could no longer endure the egotism of his liberator. This self-absorbed blowhard would not shut up. He keeps declaring, "It is I who saved you, it is I who snatched you from death." Annoyed with such pomposity, the freed person replies, "I owe nothing to you if you saved me [only] in order that you might have someone to exhibit. How long will you parade me? How long will you refuse to let me forget my misfortune? [Even if I were prisoner of war] in a triumphal procession, I should [only] have had to march but once [in shame]!" (2.11.1-2). This vivid dialogue demonstrates how benefactors could use their dependent recipients for their own ends.

This brings us to Seneca's most pertinent criticism against givers. He reprimands them for giving with purely self-interested motives. "It is a contemptible act," he exclaims,

> without praise and without glory, to do anyone a service because it is to *our own interest*. What nobleness is there in *loving oneself, in sparing oneself, in getting gain for oneself*? The true desire of giving a benefit summons us away from all these motives, and, laying hand upon us, forces us to put up with loss, and, forgoing *self-interest*, finds its greatest joy in the mere act of doing good. (4.14.3-4; my italics)

But givers are not the only ones who struggled with self-interested motives. Recipients did too. They would give return gifts in order to get bigger and better gifts from their benefactor. Seneca calls this selfish gain, not gratitude (4.17.1). Other recipients showed their gratitude toward their benefactor simply in order to get other benefactors and gain access to more gifts. But this is not how grateful people should act, says Seneca. They shouldn't show their gratitude solely to win "more friends" and obtain "more benefits." For the one who repays gratitude with "an eye on a second gift" is "ungrateful" (4.20.2-3; cf. 4.24.2).

Clearly, whether one is a giver or receiver, Seneca detests purely self-interested giving and receiving. But does that necessarily mean that he would have agreed with the modern notion of the "pure" gift? Should our giving be completely devoid of self-interest?

An ancient version of the "pure" gift? At first glance, Seneca seems to promote an ancient version of pure giving. He completely eradicates all self-interest from gift exchange. After all, his golden rule of exchange is that "the one should immediately forget that [a gift] was given, the other should never forget that [a gift] was received" (2.10.4; cf. 1.4.3, 5; 2.6.2). Forgetting implies disinterestedness, which, in turn, displays virtue. For virtue does not invite "by the prospect of *gain*." On the contrary, she "is more often found in *voluntary* contributions. We must go to her, trampling under foot *all self-interest*" (4.1.2; my italics).

Based on the words he uses, it seems as if Seneca holds to the modern distinction noted above between the *market* economy and the *gift* economy. Seneca even argues that a person must completely strip himself of self-interest if one wants to give a gift. Since a gift "has in view *only* the advantage of the recipient" (4.9.1; my italics), we are to trample "under foot *all self-interest*" (4.1.2; my italics). If Seneca took that thought to its logical conclusion, he may have arrived—like Derrida above—at the impossibility of a "pure" gift: "if there is gift held or beheld *as* gift by the other, . . . there is no gift; . . . the gift does not *exist* and does not *present* itself. If it presents itself, it no longer presents itself."[3]

Another move by Seneca makes him seem like a modern. He appeals to the way the gods give as a (pure?) model after which to pattern our giving: "God bestows upon us very many and very great benefits, *with no thought of any return*, since he has no need of having anything bestowed, nor are we capable of bestowing anything on him; consequently . . . [a benefit] has in view *only* the advantage of the recipient; so putting aside *all self-interest of our own*, let us aim *solely* at this" (4.9.1; my italics). Later, he writes, a "benefit views the interest, not of ourselves, but of the one upon whom it is bestowed; otherwise, it is to ourselves that we give it" (4.13.3).

What becomes evident from these examples, at first glance, is that self-interest should never appear in the exchange of gifts. Only disinterested givers and those who are solely concerned with the interests of others give virtuously. Although Seneca didn't use the term, we might be tempted to consider his gift-giving paradigm an ancient rendition of "pure" giving.

But that would be wrong. On closer inspection, when Seneca makes these kinds of statements, he has a very specific version of self-interest in view—the kind that exploits others for the sake of selfish gain. So, this begs the question: are *total self-interest* and *solely other-interest* the only two options when it comes to interests in giving? Seneca doesn't think so.

A virtuous other-oriented self-interest. Unlike most moderns who consider any kind of self-regard to be unethical, Seneca promotes a virtuous *other-oriented self-interest*. He writes,

> Let us never bestow benefits that can redound to our shame. Since the sum total of friendship consists in putting a friend on an equality with ourselves, *consideration must be given at the same time to the interests of both.* I shall give to him if he is in need, yet not to the extent of bringing need upon myself; I shall come to his aid if he is at the point

---

[3]"The Time of the King," in *The Logic of the Gift: Toward an Ethic of Generosity*, ed. Alan D. Schrift (New York: Routledge, 1997), 121-47 at 131; cf. also Jacques Derrida, *The Gift of Death* (Chicago: University of Chicago Press, 1995).

of ruin, yet not to the extent of bringing ruin upon myself, unless by so doing I shall purchase the safety of a great man or a great cause. (2.15.1; my italics)

The clearest example of this self- and other-regard comes later in the book:

I am not so unjust as to feel under no obligation to a man who, when *he was profitable to me, was also profitable to himself.* For I do not require that he should consult *my interests* without any regard to *his own*; no, I also desire that a benefit given to me should be even more advantageous to the giver, provided that, when he gave it, *he was considering us both, and meant to divide it between himself and me.* Though he should possess the larger part of it, provided that he allowed me to share in it, provided that he considered both of us, I am, not merely unjust, I am ungrateful, if I do not rejoice that, while he has *benefited me*, he has *also benefited himself.* (6.13.1-2; my italics)

For Seneca, profiting from giving a gift is acceptable, but only if it's done in the right way. At the moment of giving, the giver must acknowledge the interests of both parties, and the recipient must also obtain a share in the profit along with the giver. It must be mutually advantageous. But it's essential that the giver think of the recipients' interests *primarily* and his own *secondarily*. If not, it lacks virtue and cannot be considered a gift; hence, it is *other-oriented self-interest*, not the other way around.

A virtuous reciprocal obligation. If Seneca's perspective on self-interest doesn't completely distance him from the modern notion of the pure gift, his view of obligation certainly will. He never questions its existence (in fact, no one did in the ancient world). Two images helpfully capture the nature of reciprocal obligation: the three Graces (1.3.4-5) and the ball game illustration (2.17.3-7).

The three Graces are sisters in Greek mythology who joyously dance with their hands joined in a perpetual circle. They represent giving, receiving, and returning, stressing that the gift flows through each party and always returns to the giver. According to Seneca, if the cycle is anywhere broken, "the beauty of the whole is destroyed," since "it has most beauty if it is continuous and maintains an uninterrupted succession" (1.3.4). This harmonious dance emphatically highlights the virtue and obligation of reciprocity.

Seneca appeals to the ball game illustration to present a similar picture. The game is comprised of a thrower (i.e., giver) and a catcher (i.e., recipient), with the ball symbolizing a gift. The aim of the game is to keep the ball in the air. If it drops to the ground, the game is over. To keep the game going, the more skilled player must assess the skills (i.e., character) of the other person. One does so by determining whether the other player is dexterous of hand, can catch long passes or fast throws, and if one's teammate is able to throw the ball back immediately. If it is determined that the player is a novice, he or she must judge whether to go with a short, gentle lob or just place the ball directly into the other player's hand. If skilled players do not play by these rules in giving, they prove to be the cause of ingratitude in others because their gifts are impossible to catch, let alone return (2.17.5). The success of the game rests on the obligation to reciprocate or, as Seneca puts it, keeping the ball in the air.

Moving away from these illustrations, Seneca more explicitly affirms the presence of obligation in gift exchange. "The giving of a benefit is a social act," explains Seneca, "it lays someone under obligation" (5.11.5); "To return [a gift] is to give something that you owe to the one to whom it belongs when he wishes it" (7.19.2); "I am able to place a man under obligation only if he accepts; I am able to be freed from obligation only if I make a return" (7.18.2). What is intriguing about these passages is that Seneca has no qualms about transferring legally binding language of loans, such as "debt" and "obligation," to the realm of "gift." To be sure, he sharply distinguishes between gifts and loans,[4] just as moderns sharply distinguish between the market and gift economies. But, for Seneca, the virtuous social dynamic within both spheres is reciprocal obligation or gifts, on both accounts with "strings attached." The difference is that while there are

---

[4]See 3.10.2, 15.3; 5.11.4-5; 2.18.5; 3.14.2 and 3.10.1, 15.1-2; 4.39.2; 2.10.2, 31.2; 4.3.3, 13.3; 2.18.5; 3.7.1-2.

"strings attached" to gifts, they are not legally-binding strings. A person could be tried in court for refusing to pay back a loan, but no one could be taken to court for not returning a gift (3.6-17).

Circling back to our initial question then: Does Seneca promote an ancient version of the "pure" gift? The answer is an emphatic "no!" He promotes a virtuous *other-oriented self-interest* and assumes the presence of *reciprocal obligation* in gift exchange. These are the very pillars of an institution that binds society together. Without them, it will inevitably collapse.

Paul on the Modern Myth of the Pure Gift

How would Paul have responded to the modern idea of the "pure" gift? Would he have deemed it essentially Christian, or would he have criticized it for being unethical? More provocatively, when it comes to gift giving, does Paul have more in common with a pagan philosopher than with many Christians today? To arrive at answers, we need to assess his perspective on self-interest and reciprocal obligation. One may be surprised by how much commonality there is between Paul and this philosophical giant.

A Christian other-oriented self-interest? Paul steers his churches away from an ungodly self-interest, especially in Philippians. He calls out certain preachers who "proclaim Christ out of selfish ambition" (Phil 1:17) and bluntly commands the congregation to do "nothing from selfish ambition or conceit" (Phil 2:3). Instead, he promotes love as a godly antithesis to exploitative self-interest. He mentions other preachers who proclaim Christ "out of love" (Phil 1:15-16), and he also writes that "if there is . . . any comfort from love . . . complete my joy by being of the same mind, having the same love, being in full accord and of one mind" (Phil 2:2 ESV).

But what does it mean to have the "same mind" and "same love" toward one another? It involves what Philippians 2:3 commends: "in humility count others more significant than yourselves." At first glance, this verse seems to promote a primary feature of the Western "pure" gift: for a gift to be a gift, the giver must never consider his own interests but solely the interests of the one to whom he gives. In other words, it must be absolutely altruistic. It must be completely self-negating and entirely other-regarding. However, one only needs to read the next verse to discover that Paul doesn't share that post-Enlightenment perspective: "Let each of you look *not only* to his own interests, *but also* to the interests of others" (Phil 2:4). The "not only . . . but also" contrast is crucial. Self-interest is not completely eradicated from social exchange. It's radically reconfigured. The Christian ought to look to the interests of others first, while considering one's own interests second. Paul, like Seneca, approves of an *other-oriented self-interest*. The major difference, however, is that Paul roots his perspective in the Christ-event (i.e., the historical incarnation, life, death, resurrection, and ascension of Christ Jesus).

Paul writes, "Have this mind among yourselves, which is yours *in Christ Jesus*," who, in all humility, lowered himself for the sake of others; who, in all obedience, died on a cross for sinners; who, in all glory, was highly exalted by God as Lord (Phil 2:5-11 ESV; my italics). One cannot help but connect the dots here. On the basis of the context, it seems right to say that the other-oriented self-interest mentioned above also characterized the redemption accomplished by Christ. As the author of Hebrews explains, "for the joy that was set before him endured the cross" (Heb 12:2 ESV). He knew that his obedience in dependence on the Spirit would lead to exaltation and glory. But he didn't do it for that reason alone. He had the interests of his people in view as well. Jesus embodied the other-oriented self-interested mindset that is ours "in Christ Jesus," and we're called, in dependence on the Spirit and by virtue of our union with him, to do the same (Phil 2:5).

Paul then gives the church a human example of this explicitly Christian self-interest in Timothy. Hoping to send him soon, he mentions that he has "no one like him, who will be genuinely concerned for your welfare. *For they all seek their own interests, not those of Jesus Christ*" (Phil 2:20-21 ESV; my italics). The distinction here is not between self-interest and no self-interest, but between an exploitative self-interest and the interests of Jesus Christ. By including the Lord

Jesus Christ as a divine party in human relationships, he aligns our other-oriented self-interest with the interests of Christ. That means Christ governs what we are interested in, whether for ourselves or others. Or, put differently, our interestedness must be determined by our mutual relation to God in Christ. He determines what is in the best interests of both parties by his word and Spirit, and we, as his people, are called to align our interests with our Lord's.[5]

We see this exhibited in other places within this letter. In Philippians 1:21-25, Paul exhibits an other-oriented self-interest as he downplays *his own interest* "to depart and be with Christ." Why? Because it is *more advantageous for them* that he remain with them. And yet, it is also advantageous for him. His decision will result in "fruitful labor" for Paul (Phil 1:22) as well as for the community (Phil 1:25). Everyone benefits from this decision. Even Christ is magnified (Phil 1:20).

When we compare Philippians 2:30 and 4:17, we see self- and other-interest held in tension, but held together nevertheless. In 2:30, Paul mentions how Epaphroditus "nearly died for the work of Christ, risking his life to complete what was lacking in your service to me" (ESV). As a prisoner, Paul would have been utterly dependent on friends and family to provide for his material needs, since ancient prisons left prisoners to fend for themselves. Their "service" was "lacking," not because they didn't care about their apostle but because they lacked opportunity to do something about it (cf. Phil 4:10). Paul also mentions their service *to him* ("to me"), not because he seeks to exploit the community for selfish gain, but because he has a need that they, as fellow-sharers of his suffering (Phil 4:14), can meet. That is considered by Paul a godly self-interest, because, as Philippians 4:17 reveals, Paul places their interests above his own. "Not that I seek the gift [that Epaphroditus delivered], but I seek the fruit that increases to your credit" (ESV). Like Christ, Paul puts others before himself, but he nevertheless considers himself.

Paul and the Philippians share an allegiance to a common Lord who informs, guides, and manages their other-oriented self-interest

---

[5]See John M. G. Barclay, "Benefiting Others and Benefit to Oneself: Seneca and Paul on 'Altruism,'" in *Paul and Seneca in Dialogue*, ed. Joseph R. Dodson and David E. Briones, Ancient Philosophy & Religion 2 (Leiden: Brill, 2017).

toward one another. But can the same be said of reciprocal obligation? Is that Christian?

A Christian reciprocal obligation? A fundamental starting point for Paul's perspective on gift giving is Romans 11:36 ("from him and through him and to him are all things," ESV) and 1 Corinthians 4:7 ("What do you have that you did not receive?" ESV). Both texts affirm one humbling truth. All that we possess, as mere creatures, comes from our Creator God. Every gift is his, and so he determines what we do with the gifts he entrusts to our stewardship. That makes us dependent recipients who mediate divine gifts to one another. As such, reciprocal obligation is not merely between two parties, as it is for Seneca. The ties of obligation are tied into a three-way knot. Paul and the Philippians equally share a vertical tie of obligation to God and to one another. But the presence of a divine, vertical party necessarily reconfigures horizontal relationships of obligation.

No longer does one party, after giving a gift, hold the superior position over the other as the source. No longer does the recipient, after receiving a gift, become subservient to the demands of the giver. When participants exchange gifts in the divine economy, they are caught up into a divine momentum of mediation. God owns everything and gives to those in need through his people. This other-oriented movement prevents believers from hoarding gifts and so accruing social power for themselves. It also preserves relationships from degenerating into destructive competitions of one-upmanship. Instead, within this divine momentum, gifts take on a divine purpose. They are received in order to be given away and given away in order to be received, and on goes the cycle of God's grace, with God remaining the supreme giver of all gifts and the chief recipient of all gratitude.

This is precisely what takes place in Paul's gift-giving relationship with his beloved church in Philippi. He describes their relationship in Philippians 4:15 as one of "giving and receiving." Notice, it doesn't just say "giving." Nor does it just say "receiving." But "giving *and* receiving." That is Pauline shorthand for reciprocity. When we examine what their partnership (*koinōnia*) of giving *and* receiving consisted of, we quickly realize that it was obligatory.

What did Paul give, and what did the Philippians receive? Paul willingly gave the gospel of God to the Philippian church, even though he was divinely compelled to do so. "Woe to me if I do not preach the gospel!" says Paul. Why? "Because *necessity* [dare we say, obligation?] is laid upon me" (1 Cor 9:16 ESV; my italics). But this necessity extends much further than the initial preaching of the gospel. When he is torn between remaining in the flesh or departing and being with Christ (a "far better" option), he concludes that to "remain in the flesh is more *necessary* on your account" (Phil 1:23-24 ESV). He places his interests beneath theirs, and he speaks of it as "necessary" or obligatory.

But that's only one side of this reciprocal obligation. What did the Philippians give, and what did Paul receive? The Philippians gave a gift to Paul in prison through the hands of Epaphroditus (cf. Phil 2:25-30). As mentioned earlier, there was a lack in their "service" (*leitourgia*) to Paul (Phil 2:30). In the ancient world, a *leitourgia* was an obligatory task to the state, a civic duty to provide financially to those in need. Seen in that light, Paul's statement in Philippians 2:30 recalls their obligation to him. And why are they obligated to him? Because his initial gift of the gospel created a communal (*koinōnia*) relationship of reciprocal obligation—or, we could say, of "giving and receiving" (Phil 4:15).

In the economy of grace, then, gift exchange consists of giving spiritual things (i.e., the gospel) and returning physical things (i.e., money and/or provisions). This same pattern characterized the *koinōnia* between Jews and Gentiles in Romans 15. Churches from Macedonia and Achaia were "*pleased* to make some contribution for the poor among the saints at Jerusalem" (Rom 15:26 ESV; my italics). They were "pleased" rather than "forced" to do so. But just in case readers missed that point, Paul repeats himself: "they were *pleased* to do it" (Rom 15:27; my italics). Nevertheless, immediately after describing the voluntary nature of their giving, he adds, "and indeed they *owe* it to them" (Rom 15:27 ESV; my italics). Then he gives the reason they owe it to them: "if the Gentiles have come to share in their *spiritual* blessings, they ought also to be of service to them in *material* blessings" (Rom 15:27 ESV; my italics). Rather than separating the language of the marketplace from the language of gift exchange, as many moderns do, Paul has no qualms combining voluntary and obligatory language. *Koinōnia* "in Christ" entails the reciprocal obligation to exchange spiritual and material goods (cf. 1 Cor 9:11).

PAUL AND SENECA ON THE MODERN MYTH OF THE PURE GIFT

Despite their fundamental differences on theology, Paul and Seneca share a common perspective on giving and common concerns about "pure" giving. I imagine they would challenge the one-sided nature of "pure" giving. A rich benefactor who gives anonymously or a person who gives to a struggling couple and explicitly refuses reciprocity isn't simply refusing a return gift. They're refusing relationship. Gifts create and sustain reciprocal relationships. Paul and Seneca would also see more overlap between the market and gift economies. There is a virtuous or Christian version of self-interest, one that places the interests of others before one's own, but without doing away with one's own interests. The same goes for obligation. Without it, to use Seneca's ball game illustration, the game of gift exchange will be called off. Finally, Paul and Seneca would criticize the correlation between the "pure" gift and God as the purest model for giving. Although Seneca sounds like a modern when talking about the giving of the gods, he nevertheless qualifies what he means and ultimately disagrees with the logic of "pure" giving.

However, for all their points of agreement, Paul and Seneca still clash. Ironically, the fundamental difference between them lies precisely where they agree. They agree that an *other-oriented self-interest* is virtuous. They agree that *reciprocal obligation* inherently characterizes honorable forms of gift exchange. But Seneca roots those virtuous acts in reason or acting in accordance with nature, whereas Paul views them as responses to the initial grace of God in Christ by the Spirit. That is, since all things come from God and flow through us or others, we are necessarily under obligation to God to meet one another's needs. Obligation is set within a triangular relationship. And since God in Christ perfectly exemplified other-oriented self-interest in his humiliation and exaltation on behalf of his people, we are conformed to that same mindset and love for others. Under a common Lord and with his indwelling Spirit in our hearts, believers naturally look *not only* to their own interests *but also* to the interests of Christ for others. God, as Father, Son, and Holy Spirit, is the fundamental difference between Paul and Seneca. For Seneca, god is an inseparable component of one's being, but for Paul, God is a separable being who radically reconfigures human relationships. God's presence changes everything, especially the way we moderns think of self-interest, obligation, and reciprocity in gift exchange.

SIMILARITIES AND DIFFERENCES

Table 9.1. Similarities and differences

Seneca, *On Benefits*	Paul, *Philippians* and *Romans*
Seneca makes a distinction between exploitative self-interest and other-oriented self-interest.	Paul makes a distinction between ungodly self-interest and other-oriented self-interest.
Seneca assumes obligation is a virtuous element in gift giving.	Paul assumes obligation is a godly element in gift giving.
Seneca believes that the reciprocity of gifts is crucial to a well-functioning society.	Paul believes that the reciprocity of gifts is essential to the well-being of the church.
Seneca looks askance at one-way giving because it never achieves the goal of gifts: relationship.	Paul never advocates one-way giving, because *koinōnia* relationships in Christ are give-and-take relationships.
Seneca affirms other-oriented self-interest but roots it in various acts in reason and acting in accordance with nature.	Paul affirms other-oriented self-interest but roots it in the grace of God.

FOR FURTHER READING

Primary Source

Seneca. *De Beneficiis*. Translated by J. W. Basore. Cambridge, MA: Harvard University Press, 1935.

Secondary Sources

Barclay, John M. G. *Paul and the Gift*. Grand Rapids: Eerdmans, 2015.

Briones, David E. *Paul's Financial Policy: A Socio-Theological Approach*. LNTS 494. London: Bloomsbury, 2013.

Dodson, Joseph R. "New Friends and Old Rivals in the Letters of Seneca and The Epistle of Diognetus." *Perspectives in Religious Studies* 45.4 (2018): 389–405.

Engberg-Pedersen, Troels. "Gift-Giving and Friendship: Seneca and Paul in Romans 1–8 on the Logic of God's Χάρις and Its Human Response." *HTR* 101 (2008): 15-44.

Griffin, Miriam. "*De Beneficiis* and Roman Society." *JRS* 93 (2003): 92-113.

———. "Seneca's Pedagogic Strategy: *Letters* and *De Beneficiis*." In *Greek and Roman Philosophy, 100 BC – 200 AD*, edited by Richard Sorabji and Robert W. Sharples, 89-113. London: Institute of Classical Studies, 2007.

———. *Seneca on Society: A Guide to* De Beneficiis. Oxford: Oxford University Press, 2013.

Inwood, Brad. "Politics and Paradox in Seneca's *De Beneficiis*." In *Reading Seneca: Stoic Philosophy at Rome*. Oxford: Clarendon Press, 2005.

DISCUSSION QUESTIONS

1. How would you describe the *other-oriented self-interest* discussed in this chapter?

2. In what ways does Paul qualify self-interest?

3. Is Seneca correct in his assessment of ingratitude as the greatest immorality in society? Why or why not?

4. Why is it important to recognize the triangular relationship of obligation in *other-oriented self-interest* giving of gifts?

10

WHAT NO OTHER GOD COULD DO

LIFE AND AFTERLIFE AMONG PAUL AND THE PHILOSOPHERS

JAMES P. WARE

IN AN ANCIENT WORLD FILLED WITH many philosophical systems and truth claims (including the truth claim that there is no such thing as truth), Paul proclaimed Jesus Christ as the one true way. In a world of many gods and goddesses, Paul's gospel claimed to be the revelation of the one true God. Paul's gospel called upon its hearers to "[turn] to God from idols to serve a living and true God" (1 Thess 1:9).[1] This exclusive claim of Paul's good news is sometimes considered misguided or offensive in our contemporary world. Was it not intolerant on Paul's part to deny that these other gods and goddesses offered equally valid paths of salvation? But this common view is founded upon a fundamental misconception: that Paul's good news offered yet one more promise of spiritual salvation following the death of the physical body, similar to those offered by the gods of ancient worship and the divinities of the philosophers. As we will see, this is mistaken. In the world into which his gospel came, the hope Paul offered his first hearers was previously unknown. It was at the heart of the "good news" Paul had for them.

DEATH AND THE GODS IN ANTIQUITY

Among common, everyday people in the pagan world addressed by Paul's gospel, a diversity of beliefs existed regarding the soul's survival

---

[1]Scripture references throughout this chapter are the author's translation.

after the death of the body. The rejection of any kind of afterlife, the prospect of a phantom-like existence in the underworld, and the expectation of a blessed sojourn in heaven followed by the soul's reincarnation, are all well attested (see Cicero, *Tusculan Disputations* 1.27-38; Virgil, *Aeneid* 6.703-51). But all were agreed upon the impossibility of *resurrection*—the reversal of death through the restoration of the physical body to imperishable life. A typical ancient tomb inscription reads, "No one who has died rises up from here" (*Inscriptiones Graecae Urbis Romae* 3.1406). As the goddess Athena explained to Telemachus in the *Odyssey*, even the gods are powerless before the invincible power of death: "A god if he wishes can easily rescue a living man, even from afar. . . . But surely not even the gods can deliver anyone, even one they love, from death, the common fate of all" (*Odyssey* 3.229-38). "When once human beings die and the dust receives their blood," the god Apollo proclaims in Aeschylus's tragedy entitled the *Eumenides*, "there can be no resurrection. All other things his mighty power can do or undo with effortless ease, but for death alone my father Zeus has no divine enchantment" (*Eumenides* 647-49). The inescapable fate of death for all mortals was a necessity even the gods were powerless to alter.

THE PHILOSOPHERS ON DEATH AND THE AFTERLIFE

The philosophers, like the general populace, held a variety of views regarding the possibility of life after death. The Epicureans believed that the soul perished together with the body (Lucretius, *On the Nature of the Universe* 3; Philodemus, *On Death* 1, 19, 20, 26, 28-32). Plato and his followers maintained that the soul after death passes into the body of an entirely new person and, over infinite time, into the bodies of numberless different persons (or animals), in an eternal cycle or wheel of death and reincarnation (e.g., Plato, *Phaedrus* 247-49; see also *Bhagavad Gita* 2.12-22; Gautama Buddha, *Anguttara Nikāya* 3.58-61, 103-5). The Stoics took differing positions. For some, whether the soul survived the death of the body or not was an open question (e.g., Seneca, *Epistles* 102). However, most Stoics held that the soul lived on in the celestial regions, but only for a limited time, and then perished (Cicero, *Tusculan Disputations* 1.77; Diogenes Laertius, *Lives* 7.157).

But (like the common people) the philosophers were in agreement on the impossibility of resurrection—return from bodily death to an everlasting embodied life. The closest analogue among the philosophers to the concept of resurrection was the Stoic doctrine of "recurrence." This doctrine postulated the cyclical destruction by fire and subsequent renewal, in its identical form, of the entire created order (Epictetus, *Disc.* 3.13.4-7; Cicero, *On the Nature of the Gods* 2.118; Seneca, *Ep.* 9.16; 36.10-11; 71.11-16). According to the Stoic teaching, the embodied life and death of each individual (but without conscious awareness of his or her past lives) would also be replicated in an endless cycle. But this notion of recurrence is very different from the hope of resurrection. Resurrection involves the miraculous return to bodily life of the same person, never to die again, the conscious renewal and continuation of personal and bodily identity. The doctrine of recurrence affirms death's eternal role in the cosmic scheme. It does not envision a time when bodily death will be no more. In the Stoic teaching, as in the other ancient philosophic visions of the cosmic future, death is a permanent fixture of the cosmos, and for every person it is irreversible and everlasting.

THE PHILOSOPHERS ON DEALING WITH DEATH

People in the ancient world did not regard death with indifference. To the contrary, the poet Lucretius informs us that, for his contemporaries, the fear of death "overturns all of human life, tainting all things with the blackness of death, and allowing no pleasure to be free from care and unalloyed" (*On the Nature of the Universe* 3.37-40). The philosophers differed from the average person in that they sought a systematic and reasoned way of coping with this fear.

An example of the way the philosophers sought to do this is provided by the Stoic philosopher Seneca (a contemporary of Paul). Seneca believed that the chief aim of the wise person was to banish "the dread of death shared by every human being" (*Ep.* 82; see also 4.3-9; 22.14-17; 24.6-18; 26.5-10; 30.3-17; 54.4-7; 91.18-21). Dispelling this fear was the chief aim of his work *On Providence*. As the title of the work implies, the Stoics believed in divine providence. Their understanding of the divine was a mix of pantheism and polytheism. They acknowledged the gods of ancient polytheistic worship, but conceived among the many gods a single highest divinity, who governed all things with reason and wisdom. And yet they did not conceive this divinity as outside nature and the cosmos, but identified God with the material universe and the rational human soul in each person (Zeno of Citium, in *Stoicorum Veterum Fragmenta* 1.163; Seneca, *Ep.* 92.30; 120.14). In the climactic passage of *On Providence*, this divinity is speaking to humanity:

> I have placed every good within you; your good fortune is not to need good fortune. "But," you say, "many sad things, frightful and hard to bear, happen to us." Because I was unable to keep you from these sufferings, I have armed you against them all—endure bravely! This is the way in which you may be superior to God: the divinity is without sufferings, you are above them. Disregard poverty: no one lives as poor as he was born. Disregard pain: it will either go away or take you away. Disregard death: it either brings you to an end or to a different place. Disregard fortune: I have given it no weapon with which it can strike your soul. Before all things I have taken care that nothing should hold you in life if you are unwilling: the exit lies open. . . . Let every time, every place teach you how easy it is to renounce nature and thrust its gift of life back in its face! (*Prov.* 6.5-8)

The words of the divinity in *On Providence* 6.5 express the fundamental Stoic conviction in their endeavor to cope with death: suffering and death are not evils. For the wise person, they are a matter of indifference. However, the words of the divinity that follow in 6.6 reflect a crucial qualification: "because *I was unable* to keep you from these sufferings, I have armed you against them all." The words "I was unable" reflect a conception involving definite limits to the power of the divinity and the goodness of creation. In Stoic thought, the necessity of fleshly embodiment, given its inherent perishability, placed constraints even on divine providence and power (see Epictetus, *Disc.* 1.1.10-12; Seneca, *Ep.* 58.27; 107.9-10). Physical evils, suffering, and death, although not the purpose of God in creation, are thus the concomitant, or unavoidable byproduct, of that purpose. This view of the cosmos is in the last analysis a tragic one, in which suffering and death are woven by necessity into the fabric of the universe, beyond the ability of even the highest divinity to forestall.

What are the practical implications of this conception of divine powerlessness in the face of death? The imperative that follows the divinity's explanation of the origin of suffering and death is crucial for grasping Seneca's perspective: "endure bravely!" (*Prov.* 6.6). Seneca counseled noble *resignation* or *acquiescence* to death, a necessity that even the highest divinity was unable to alter (see also Seneca, *Ep.* 4.5; 30.4; 36.11; 49.10; 71.16; 91.18; 94.6-8; 107.9-10). The Stoic teaching often went beyond mere acquiescence to an active embrace of death. Seneca and his fellow Stoics approved, even encouraged, suicide under the proper circumstances (see Seneca, *Ep.* 70; 77; 120.14-15; Cicero, *On Final Ends* 3.60-61; Epictetus, *Disc.* 1.2.25-28). We see this in *On Providence* 6.8 above, which extols how easy it is, through suicide, to "renounce nature and thrust its gift of life back in its face!"

For Seneca, death is the everlasting sorrow, and the wise conform themselves to this reality through noble resignation or active embrace of death. In Seneca's Stoic philosophy, as in each of the major philosophical views in antiquity, suffering and death were understood as belonging to the very essence of the universe, an irreversible and everlasting feature of the cosmic order. The gods of the ancient pagan world, whether the philosophic divinities or the gods of popular worship, were powerless before the unconquerable might of death.

A DIFFERENT GOD AND HIS PROMISED VICTORY

Within this ancient context, the one God worshipped by the Jewish people was not only a different God, but a different *kind* of God altogether. For the varied gods of the pagan world were either (as in Stoicism) identified with the cosmos, or (as in ancient polytheism, Epicureanism, and Buddhism) considered products or aspects of it, or (as in Platonism) believed to coexist alongside an independent and eternal material realm. Both the gods of ancient worship and the philosophic divinities were accordingly limited in their powers.

In starkest contrast, the ancient Jews believed that their God, the God of Israel, was the transcendent Creator (Is 40:12-31; Jer 10:1-16; Amos 5:8; Ps 33:6-9; 95:1-7; 124:8). He was unlimited in his power (Gen 18:14; Jer 32:17; Ps 135:5-6), and the cosmos was his good and perfect handiwork (Gen 1–2; Ps 104; 148). Death was not a necessary byproduct of creation, but the result of the fall and the curse (Gen 3). And the Jewish people awaited a coming kingdom and reign of God, when the God of Israel would reveal himself as the one true God by doing what only the almighty creator God could do—he would *defeat death forever*. The book of Isaiah envisions the coming of the Lord to Mount Zion, the holy city Jerusalem, to redeem all nations:

> And on this mountain the Lord of hosts will prepare for all the peoples a feast of rich foods, a feast of aged wines, of choicest rich foods, of finest aged wines. And he will swallow up on this mountain the burial cloth which covers all the peoples, the mourning veil which veils all the nations—he will swallow up death forever! And the Lord God will wipe away tears from all faces, and will remove the reproach of his people from all the earth, for the Lord has spoken. And it will be said in that day, "Behold, here is our God! We put our hope in him, and he has saved us. Here is the Lord! We put our hope in him; let us rejoice and be glad in his salvation." (Is 25:6-9)

Moreover, the Jewish Scriptures foretell a renewal of all creation, when the wolf will lie down with the lamb, and the glory of the Lord will fill the whole earth, as the waters cover the sea (Is 11:6-9; 65:25; 66:22-24; Amos 9:13). In the midst of an ancient world that believed even the gods had no authority over the realm of death, the Jewish people awaited a new act of God, whereby death would be undone, and the whole created order would be restored and renewed.

PAUL'S EASTER GOSPEL

It was into this world that Paul brought "the good news of Jesus and of his resurrection" (Acts 17:18). He proclaimed that "Christ is risen from the dead" (1 Cor 15:20). In proclaiming that Jesus had been raised, Paul was not merely claiming that Jesus' death had been followed by some form of afterlife. Instead, Jesus' death had been *reversed* through his restoration, three days after his death and burial, to full bodily life. Jesus' once-dead body, the body of flesh and bones laid in the tomb, had been raised to life and made imperishable. Paul's gospel announced *the restoration to life of Jesus' crucified body*, an event within the space-time universe, verified by eyewitness testimony:

> For I transmitted to you from the first, which I also received, that Christ died for our sins in fulfillment of the Scriptures, and that he was buried, and that he was raised on the third day in fulfillment of the Scriptures, and that he was seen by Peter, then by the twelve apostles; then he was seen by more than five hundred brothers and sisters at the same time, of whom the majority remain until now, but some have fallen asleep; then he was seen by James, then by all the apostles; and last of all, as to one born out of due time, he was seen by me as well. (1 Cor 15:3-8)

This brings us to the crux of Paul's understanding of Jesus' resurrection and the heart of Paul's gospel. According to Paul's "good news," Jesus not only suffered and died "for us" (1 Thess 5:10; cf. Titus 2:14) but also *rose again* "for us" (2 Cor 5:15; cf. Rom 4:24-25; 8:34). And therefore *when he rose from the dead, Jesus conquered death on behalf of all humanity*. He had done what the prophets promised the God of Israel would do in the time of his coming kingdom and reign. He had undone the ancient curse. Jesus had "abolished death, and brought to us the light of life and incorruptibility, through the good news" (2 Tim 1:10). Paul's gospel announced that in Jesus' resurrection, death itself, humanity's great enemy, had been conquered by the creator God:

> But now Christ is risen from the dead, the first fruits of those who are asleep. For since death came through a human being, the resurrection of the dead came through a human being. For just as in Adam all die,

so in Christ all will be made alive. But each in his own order; Christ the first fruits, then those who belong to Christ at his coming. Then comes the consummation, when he delivers over the kingdom to his God and Father, when he abolishes all opposing rule, and all authority and power. For Jesus must reign as king until the Father puts all things under his feet. The last enemy that will be abolished is death. (1 Cor 15:20-26)

Paul proclaims in this passage that in Jesus' resurrection the promised conquest of death has now come, but in a way involving two distinct phases or stages. The first stage is Jesus' own resurrection. Jesus is the "first fruits" of the harvest, anticipating the full harvest to come (1 Cor 15:20). And according to Paul's gospel, the power of Christ's resurrection life is already at work in those who believe. Through baptism into Jesus' death and resurrection, believers enter into a supernatural and transforming union with God's Son, freeing them from the power of sin and from demonic enslavement (Rom 6:1-11; 1 Cor 6:9-11; 2 Cor 3:17-18; Eph 4:17-24; Phil 3:9-10; Titus 3:3-7). Those who die in Christ are only "asleep" (1 Cor 15:20), their bodies waiting to be awakened on the day of Christ, and in the interim their souls or spirits are "with Christ" (Phil 1:20-24) in heaven, "away from the body but present with the Lord" (2 Cor 5:6-8). But the full outworking of Jesus' life-giving resurrection awaits the second stage, his future coming in glory, when all those who belong to Christ will be raised to imperishable bodily life (1 Cor 15:23-26).

First Corinthians 15:20-26 reveals crucial differences between the thought of Seneca and of Paul. In contrast with Seneca's limited deity, identified with the cosmos, Paul's God is the God of Israel, the almighty Creator, who created all things from nothing (see also Rom 1:20-23; 4:17; 1 Cor 8:4-6; Eph 3:9; Col 1:16-17; 1 Tim 6:13). The cosmos is not God but God-given, the direct creative act of a holy Creator, and thus endowed with an indelible goodness and sacredness ("the earth is the Lord's and its fullness," 1 Cor 10:26). But Paul also believes in an event within creation's history, leading to a tragic disruption of this good created order. Through the rebellion of humanity, death entered the cosmos (1 Cor 15:21-22), and the world was enslaved to malevolent spiritual powers opposed to God and hostile to humanity (1 Cor 15:24-25).

We find ourselves here at a crux point of difference between the thought of Seneca and of Paul. For Seneca, bodily death is a tragic but inescapable defect within the created order, a necessary byproduct of creation itself, beyond the power of even the highest divinity to undo. According to Paul's gospel, evil, suffering, and death are *enemies* (1 Cor 15:25-26), intruders into the good creation, due not to limitations upon God, the almighty and good Creator, but to cosmic and human rebellion. For Seneca, the cosmos is a world by necessity ill-made; for Paul, the cosmos is a good world marred, ruined, or spoiled. But through Jesus' resurrection the Creator has now reclaimed his creation. The death that infects the creation has been vanquished through Jesus' life-creating resurrection, and it will be abolished at his coming in glory (1 Cor 15:20, 23, 26).

EASTER INAUGURATED AND CONSUMMATED

Paul's gospel not only announced Jesus' resurrection as the fulfillment of the scriptural promise of the creator God's victory over death, but also looked forward in hope to the day when he would bring that victory to full consummation:

> Behold, I tell you a mystery: we shall not all sleep, but we shall all be changed. In a moment of time, in the twinkling of an eye, at the final trumpet: for the trumpet will sound, and the dead will be raised imperishable, and we shall be changed. For this perishable body must clothe itself with imperishability, and this mortal body must clothe itself with immortality. And when this perishable body clothes itself with imperishability, and this mortal body clothes itself with immortality, then will come to pass the word which stands written: "Death has been swallowed up in victory!" (1 Cor 15:51-54)

Paul's final words in the passage above, "Death has been swallowed up in victory," are taken from the passage from Isaiah quoted earlier, which envisions the coming of God to destroy death, judge the wicked who oppose God, and put an end to suffering and sorrow. Moreover, according to Paul's gospel, the full outworking of Christ's resurrection would bring to pass the fulfillment of the scriptural promises of the creator God's renewal of the entire created order:

> But if we are God's children, we are also heirs; heirs of God, and fellow heirs with Christ, if indeed we suffer with him that we may also be glorified with him. For I consider that the sufferings of this present age are not worthy to be compared with the glory which will be revealed to us. For the longing expectation of the creation eagerly awaits the revelation of the children of God. For the created order was subjected to futility, not of its own accord but because of the will of God who subjected it, in the hope that *the creation itself will be set free from its slavery to decay, to share in the freedom of the glory of the children of God*. (Rom 8:17-21, italics added)

In the coming consummation, Paul's gospel proclaimed, all things will be made new, death will be swallowed up in victory, and the entire creation filled with the glory of the Lord. In Seneca's philosophy, death is the necessary byproduct of creation and will exist forever in an everlasting cyclical recurrence of all things. In Paul's teaching, death is the baneful distortion of the good creation, but has now been overthrown by Jesus' resurrection from the dead, and at his coming in glory will be no more. In contrast with the philosophy of Seneca (and of Plato and Epicurus), which was *life-negating*, Paul's good news of Jesus' resurrection is *life-affirming*. It affirms the transcendent value, goodness, sacredness, and permanence of *this* world and of *this* body. "The body is not for sexual immorality but for the Lord, and the Lord for the body. God raised up the Lord, and will raise us up by his power" (1 Cor 6:13-14). It affirms the ultimate victory of life over death. Jesus did not divest himself of his human body, born of the Virgin Mary (Rom 1:3-4; Gal 4:4). Rather, in the resurrection, Jesus' body was *glorified* (Rom 6:4; Phil 3:21), and the glorification of Jesus' body is the first fruits of the glorification and final perfection of the whole created order (1 Cor 15:20-28).

All this leads to a striking difference in the character of the present life to which Seneca and Paul call their readers. For Seneca, death is the ultimate reality, and the chief aim of the wise person is to banish the fear of his own demise and meet death with brave resignation. In Paul's letters, the ancient philosophical vocabulary of resignation and acquiescence with regard to death is strikingly absent; in its place we find an astonishingly pervasive vocabulary of *hope, expectancy, joy,* and *thanksgiving,* centered on the new and living hope brought by Jesus' resurrection from the dead (Rom 5:2-5; 8:24-25; 12:12; 15:13; Phil 4:4-7; 1 Thess 5:8, 16-18).

Conclusion: Good News and a Summons

To an ancient world for which death was the eternal sorrow, unconquerable either by the gods of ancient worship or the divinities of the philosophers, the resurrection of Jesus' crucified body from the tomb brought the good news of the creator God's victory over death. In conquering death, Jesus had done what none of the gods of the pagan world could do, or even claimed to do, and therefore revealed himself as the true living God. And that is why Paul's gospel was both an announcement of good news and a summons to conversion from false gods to the one true God. This gospel demanded a decision and a response. Easter was not only good news, replacing the everlasting sorrow of the pagan world into which Paul's gospel came with the joyous hope of the resurrection. Easter was the revelation of the identity of the one true God.

For Further Reading

Primary Sources
Cicero. *Tusculan Disputations.* Translated by J. E. King. LCL. London: Harvard University Press, 2001.

Seneca. *Moral Essays.* Translated by John W. Basore. LCL. London: Harvard University Press, 2003.

Secondary Sources
Malherbe, Abraham. *Paul and the Popular Philosophers.* Minneapolis: Fortress, 1989.

Mansfeld, Jaap. "Providence and the Destruction of the Universe in Early Stoic Thought." In *Studies in Hellenistic Religions*, edited by J. Vermaseren, 160-88. Leiden: Brill, 1979.

Ware, James P. *Paul's Theology in Context: Creation, Incarnation, Covenant, and Kingdom*. Grand Rapids: Eerdmans, 2019.

———. "Paul's Understanding of the Resurrection in 1 Corinthians 15:36-54." *JBL* 133 (2014): 809-35.

———. "The Salvation of Creation: Seneca and Paul on the Cosmos, Human Beings, and their Future." In *Paul and Seneca in Dialogue*, edited by Joseph R. Dodson and David E. Briones, 285-306, Ancient Philosophy and Religion Series 2. Leiden/Boston: Brill, 2017.

Wright, N. T. *The Resurrection of the Son of God*. Minneapolis: Fortress, 2003.

DISCUSSION QUESTIONS

1. According to this chapter, was Paul's gospel of the resurrection of Jesus a new message for his hearers? Why or why not?

2. What differences between 1 Corinthians 15 and Seneca's *On Providence* did you find most striking?

3. In what way was Paul's message both a proclamation of good news and at the same time a challenge and a summons?

4. Did the context of the ancient pagan world into which Paul's gospel came, as illumined by this chapter, help you to better understand Paul's gospel? If so, in what way?

11

SOMEWHERE OVER THE RAINBOW

HEAVENLY VISIONS IN PLATO, CICERO, AND PAUL

JOSEPH R. DODSON

THE APOSTLE PETER ONCE ADMITTED that Paul writes some things that are hard to understand and difficult to interpret (2 Pet 3:16). Although Peter resists stating what perplexing passage he has in mind, 2 Corinthians 12:1-8 would have been a good case in point. In this section where Paul is boasting yet not really boasting, bragging but only *humble*-bragging, he writes:

> I must go on boasting. Although there is nothing to be gained, I will go on to visions and revelations from the Lord. I know a man in Christ who fourteen years ago was caught up to the third heaven. Whether it was in the body or out of the body I do not know—God knows. And I know that this man—whether in the body or apart from the body I do not know, but God knows—was caught up to paradise and heard inexpressible things, things that no one is permitted to tell. I will boast about a man like that, but I will not boast about myself, except about my weaknesses. Even if I should choose to boast, I would not be a fool, because I would be speaking the truth. But I refrain, so no one will think more of me than is warranted by what I do or say, or because of these surpassingly great revelations. Therefore, in order to keep me from becoming conceited, I was given a thorn in my flesh, a messenger of Satan, to torment me. (2 Cor 12:1-7)

First of all, who is this "man in Christ"? Is Paul talking about himself or someone else? If he is talking about himself, why does he do so in the third person? Does it matter whether he was caught up "in the body"? If not, why does he mention it twice (vv. 2, 3)? Also why isn't the man permitted to tell what he heard? What made the words "inexpressible" in the first place? Were they in some sort of heavenly language? And what about that "thorn in the flesh"? Why doesn't Paul tell us what (or who) it is? Wait, did God actually send a messenger of *Satan* to torment Paul? Questions abound.

While this passage is peculiar for Paul, it's not without parallel. There are numerous examples from the Old Testament and other Jewish texts where a special person is caught up into heaven and experiences supernatural visions. Of these, the one you are probably most familiar with is the Book of Revelation. Such works like Revelation and specific passages like 2 Corinthians 12:1-8 are often referred to as apocalyptic texts.

Although scholars have been engaged in a perennial battle over what exactly defines "apocalyptic," many of them probe Jewish parallels to help them decipher passages where Paul delves into apocalyptic discussions, however defined. And rightly so! I can't tell you how much these scholars have helped me understand Paul's letters better in light of this aspect of his Jewish background. But Jewish apocalypticism isn't the only parallel that illumines Paul's thinking. There are *also* similarities between these passages in Paul and two philosophical titans in the ancient world, Plato and Cicero. They crown their capital works with stories about a person raptured away to paradise who sees incredible visions and hears mystical messages. A comparative chapter could barely ask for anything better.

Plato and Cicero's works would have been known by at least some believers in the Corinthian church (similar to how many in your church would be familiar with the story of Dorothy being caught up to Oz). Whether intentionally or not, these stories could have influenced how original readers interpreted Paul's letters, not least 2 Corinthians 12:1-8. Therefore, let's look at these two ancient accounts of people being caught up to paradise before comparing them to Paul's experience.

Plato's *Republic* and the Myth of Er

According to N. T. Wright, Plato's works are like the New Testament of the ancient Hellenistic world.[1] Within this "Hellenistic New Testament," Plato tells the story of Er to conclude his book, the *Republic*. The philosopher uses the story to illustrate the lasting importance for people to live right and practice justice (Plato, *Resp.* 10.614d-619b). Plato seeks to demonstrate that despite how great the prizes, gifts, and rewards a righteous person might receive here on earth, they fail to compare—in both number and magnitude—with what awaits them after death (Plato, *Resp.* 10.614a).

As the story goes, Er is a valiant warrior who dies in battle. After he is slain, it takes his friends twelve days to find his body, deliver it home, and prepare for the funeral. On that last day, his loved ones place Er's corpse on a pyre to incinerate it. And yet, as they are getting ready to light it on fire, Er sits up. He shocks the crowd by coming back to life. Have you ever wondered what Lazarus or Jairus's daughter told their loved ones after each of them came back from the dead? Well, in contrast to these biblical examples, Er actually details what he saw "in the world beyond."

According to Er, at the beginning of his twelve-day journey in the afterlife, the judges gathered him together with the other departed souls around the judgment seat. But over against the rest, Er gets a pass. Rather than remaining with the dead, the judges appoint him to take a look around and take notes so that he can go back and give a report to humanity regarding the destiny of the dead. Er then watches as the judges separate the wicked souls from the righteous ones, to the left and to the right (Plato, *Resp.* 10.614c-d). The just souls, who are sent to the right, journey into heaven where they experience inexpressible joy and ceaseless delights for one thousand years. In contrast to the righteous party in paradise, the unjust souls on the left suffer nightmarish torments for that whole time under the earth where they repay tenfold the sins they committed in life (Plato, *Resp.*

---

[1]N. T. Wright, *The Resurrection of the Son of God* (Minneapolis: Fortress, 2003), 32, 47-48.

10.615a-616a). When Er returns to his body, then, he proclaims what he saw in order to persuade people to seek righteousness so that they may avoid infernal torment on the one hand and reap heavenly rewards on the other (Plato, *Resp.* 10.619e; 621c-d).

As we will see below, this tale of Er left a lasting impression on another giant of philosophy, Marcus Tullius Cicero.

Cicero's *Republic* and the Dream of Scipio

Just as Plato concludes his book with the myth of Er, Cicero punctuates his *Republic* with the dream of Scipio. While Plato does so to encourage people to pursue justice, Cicero uses Scipio's story to dissuade his disgruntled peers from abandoning their office due to Rome's toxic political environment.[2] As history would go on to show, Cicero was in a losing battle to keep his republic ruled by the people instead of the vainglorious emperors who would inevitably ensue. For Cicero, however, there was more at stake than losing the soul of Rome. His vision warns that those who forfeit their responsibility to rule their nation will also forfeit their hope for immortality in the age to come.

Similar to how Jesus refers to Jonah's return to life after three days in the fish as a way to introduce his imminent resurrection from the grave, Scipio uses the story of Er's rapture to introduce his own heavenly vision. Cicero draws from Er and Scipio's experience to demonstrate that the doctrines of heaven and the soul's immortality should not be scorned. They aren't fables and fairy tales to be laughed at; they're rational teachings to be considered. "The things that are told of the immortality of the soul and of the heavens [are not] the fictions of dreaming philosophers, or such incredible tales as the Epicureans mock at, but the conjectures of sensible men" (Cicero, *Resp.* 6.3).

Scipio's story begins with him telling how, on a military expedition, a deceased war-hero called Africanus appears to him in a dream. At the sight of the specter, Scipio shudders with fright, but Africanus gets

---

[2]Pheme Perkins, *Resurrection* (New York: Doubleday, 1984).

right to business. He says, "Be courageous, Scipio, do not be afraid. Imprint the words I am about to say to you on your memory" (Cicero, *Resp.* 6.10; my translation).

Africanus then proceeds to prophesy about Scipio's future victories for Rome and to foretell how the republic will be disturbed by selfish politicians. He goes on to say to Scipio:

> Be assured of this, so that you may be even more eager to defend the commonwealth: all those who have preserved, aided, or enlarged the fatherland have a special place prepared for them in the heavens, where they may enjoy an eternal life of happiness. For nothing of all that is down on earth is more pleasing to that supreme God who rules the whole universe than the assemblies and gatherings of men associated in justice. (Cicero, *Resp.* 6.13; LCL)

But even with Africanus standing before him, Scipio still has doubts as to whether life after death truly exists. Africanus responds: "Surely all those you consider to be dead are alive. Like an inmate from a prison, they have escaped from the bondage of the body. In contrast, however, what you call 'life' is really death" (Cicero, *Resp.* 6.14; my translation). In other words, Scipio's current biological life is death compared to the spiritual life that is to come. It is only when the righteous die that they obtain life that is truly life.

To rid Scipio of his skepticism, Africanus summons Scipio's deceased father, Paulus, to join them. Scipio weeps as his dad approaches to embrace him (Cicero, *Resp.* 6.15). Now that he is reunited with his father, Scipio doesn't ever want to go back to earth. He begs his dad to let him leave his life below so that he can stay with his father in heaven forever. Paulus solemnly informs Scipio that he must return to his body, since only God, the author of life, has the prerogative to give one leave of their duty on earth (Cicero, *Resp.* 6.15). Scipio cannot therefore shirk his responsibility to his republic. Rather, he must imitate his father by cultivating justice in the world. But the good news is that once Scipio spreads goodwill and righteousness on earth, he will be able to return to heaven when he "dies" to dwell with the righteous forever (Cicero, *Resp.* 6.16).

At this point, Scipio begins to describe the details of all that he sees in the heavens. He describes sights wonderfully beautiful and bright—everywhere he turns as far as his eyes can see. Eventually, Scipio looks down and surveys the earth and is startled by how dwarfed it is in comparison to the Milky Way (Cicero, *Resp.* 6.16). So awestruck at the planets and the stars nearest him, Scipio fails to notice what's most impressive. Thus, Africanus redirects Scipio's gaze to "the nine spheres of heaven." The last of which is where "the Supreme God dwells" (Cicero, *Resp.* 6.17).

Rather than leading Scipio to the throne room of God, however, Africanus begins to preach. He expounds on how foolish it is for anyone to pursue fame in light of the grand scheme of things: God, history, and the stars. Since cosmic fires and earthly floods will wipe everything away, no person will ever gain enduring glory or everlasting fame. All human boasts will be forgotten when the world ends and the stars return to their original configuration (Cicero, *Resp.* 6.23-24). For this reason, rather than seeking vain and evanescent glory, Scipio should seek the things above and set his heart upon heaven. That's where he will find his everlasting reward (Cicero, *Resp.* 6.20-25). Fixing his mind on his final resting place will enable him to ignore the vulgar herd around him so that virtue can lead him to *true* glory (Cicero, *Resp.* 6.25). Therefore, in light of this hope, Scipio must stay committed to the best pursuits and detach himself from earthly pleasures. Fighting for justice while focusing on heaven, before long, he will ascend to the soul's proper home (Cicero, *Resp.* 6.29).

Before Scipio's vision ends, he gets a glimpse of the consequences he will suffer if he fails to live a virtuous life. When the wretched die, rather than flying to heaven, they are bound to the ground—where they endure most incredible torments for many ages in order to pay for breaking the laws of men and of God (Cicero, *Resp.* 6.29).

In sum, as we have seen so far, Plato and Cicero employ the myth of Er and the dream of Scipio to underscore that virtuous souls ascend to heaven when they die, while wicked souls will be dreadfully tortured for their sins. In both stories, a hero is caught up to experience a higher form of life beyond this biological existence. While Er has judges telling him to record what he sees about judgment—heaven and hell—Scipio has Africanus and Paulus meet him to prophesy about the future and to give him a tour of the stars.

PLATO AND CICERO AND PAUL

Before specifically comparing 2 Corinthians 12:1-8 to the accounts of Scipio and Er, let's look at some of the parallels and differences between them in light of Paul's letters in general. For example, all three of these authors express hope for a better life after death. Their basis of this hope centers on ascension stories. As we saw above, Plato uses the tale of Er to highlight how the bounty and boons righteous people receive in this world pale in comparison to the blessings they'll get in the next (Plato, *Resp.* 10.614a). Similarly, according to Africanus, what mortals consider life is really death compared to the glorious life reserved for the virtuous in heaven.

This somewhat coheres with Paul's proclamation that our temporary life and all its sufferings are light compared to the eternal weighted glory of God, in which believers will fully share in the next age (2 Cor 4:17; Rom 8:16-18). One of the major differences, however, is that whereas Plato and Cicero looked forward to their reward at the moment of their *bodily death*, Paul concentrates the hope of believers on the day of their *bodily resurrection*. And, just as significant, Plato and Cicero's hope of everlasting life depends on individual virtue (if you're good enough, you'll make it), whereas Paul's hope centers—not on our works—but on the righteous act of Jesus Christ. The Lord's one righteous deed resulted in life for all people, and through his one act of obedience, the many will be made righteous (Rom 5:18-19).

Related to this point, while Plato and Cicero draw their understandings of the soul's afterlife from the stories of Er and Scipio, Paul bases his belief in everlasting life on the resurrection of his Messiah (1 Cor 15:20). Since believers have been buried with Christ by baptism into his death, they have assurance that they will be united with him in resurrection (Rom 6:1-11). Therefore, similar to the hopes of Scipio, before too long the believers will see their departed loved ones again (1 Thess 4:14). Soon the dead in Christ will rise from the tomb and soar into the skies (1 Thess 4:13-14). After that, the rest of the believers will follow them to meet Christ in the air (1 Thess 4:17). The Spirit will give life to their mortal bodies (Rom 8:11), which will be transformed in the twinkling of an eye (1 Cor 15:51-52). This brings us to yet another fundamental difference between Paul and the philosophers. Plato and Cicero concern themselves with the fate of *individuals* at their deaths, but the apostle focuses on the *large group*—the entire community of believers at the final resurrection.

Similar to Scipio's longing to depart from his body to be with his father in heaven, Paul confesses that he prefers to be away from his body so that he can be with the Lord. Whereas Scipio resolves to stay for the benefit of Rome, the apostle resigns to remain in his body for the sake of the church (Phil 1:23-25). On another note, as with Scipio and Er, Paul encourages people to live righteously because everyone will give an account for their actions done in the body (Rom 14:10-12; 2 Cor 5:9-10). Yet in another contrast, Paul believes that not only will humanity's deeds be judged, but their secret thoughts and motives will be as well (Rom 2:16; 1 Cor 4:5).

As with Plato and Cicero, Paul promises heavenly rewards for the righteous and warns of coming judgment for transgressors and lawbreakers. But whereas the philosophers specifically refer to postmortem torment for the wicked, Paul actually never mentions a resurrection of the unrighteous dead, nor does he detail what happened to the depraved souls who have already departed. Rather, the apostle seems content merely to say that the wicked will not inherit the kingdom. Consequently, God's wrath is *already* being revealed from heaven upon them, and ruin will soon sweep them away (Rom 1:17-18; 1 Cor 6:9-11; 1 Thess 5:3). The apostle does not therefore mention any tortuous incarceration for a thousand years like we saw in the tale of Er or of deceased lawbreakers suffering for countless years as we read about in Scipio's dream. This brings us back to the curious passage in 2 Corinthians 12.

Conclusion: Er, Scipio, and the Man in Christ in 2 Corinthians 12

Similar to the accounts in Plato and Cicero, Paul tells a story of a person who was caught up to heaven (2 Cor 12:1-4).[3] As with the cases of Scipio and Er, the heavenly ascent of the "man" provides a preview of the world to come. In stark contrast, however, Plato and Cicero rely on secondhand accounts—tales passed down to them. But, if the general consensus is correct, Paul gives an *eyewitness account*. That is to say, most scholars believe that the "man in Christ" is Paul referring to himself, albeit in a roundabout way. Therefore, Paul himself is the man who was caught up to heaven. It may seem weird to us for Paul to speak in this fashion, but it's his maneuver of boasting while not boasting.[4]

As mentioned above, another peculiarity in this passage is Paul's repeated mention of his ignorance as to whether he was in the body or not. In comparison to Plato and Cicero, it could be that his revelation was more like Scipio's dream (in the body), or perhaps more akin to Er's post-mortem experience (out of it). If it is similar to Er's account, maybe Paul's revelation was a result of one of his own near death experiences. For example, just before our text, Paul lists many of his afflictions in 2 Corinthians 11:23, noting that he had been exposed to death time and again.

While Paul is uncertain about how he got up to paradise, he is sure about one thing: he cannot repeat what he heard while he was there. Thus, over against the purpose of Scipio's vision to spur him on so that he redoubles his efforts to serve Rome, on the surface Paul's revelation seems to reveal nothing. The apostle is not permitted to share any

---

[3]The ideas in this section are expanded in Joseph R. Dodson, "The Transcendence of Death and Heavenly Ascent in the Apocalyptic Paul and the Stoics" in *Paul and the Apocalyptic Imagination*, edited by Ben C. Blackwell, John K. Goodrich, and Jason Maston (Minneapolis: Fortress, 2016), 168-70.

[4]There is an ancient, non-Christian example of this kind of boasting. In *On Inoffensive Self-Praise*, Plutarch says it is okay for people to boast, as long as they do so in the right way and for the right reason. They can boast about their virtue for the sake of inspiring others to follow their example and so keep them from emulating evil and adopting bad philosophies. Nevertheless, this kind of boasting must be indirect, giving credit to God, praise to the audience, and admitting personal shortcomings. One can easily detect many similarities with Paul's boast in 2 Cor 12.

details of what he saw. Presumably, even if he tried to tell what he heard, he couldn't—due to the "inexpressible words." Consequently, while the ascent stories of Er and Scipio feed people's spiritual hunger to know more about the afterlife, Paul's account is a meager *hors d'oeuvre*, barely even a starter.

Further, a heavenly mediator was a common feature in apocalyptic accounts. Following suit, Er mentions judges who met him to give him instructions, and Scipio had two celestial guides to help him in his journey. (Even John has an angel in Revelation to lead him.) But Paul makes no mention of such a figure. Was there anyone in paradise to help him understand? If so, was it this unmentioned helper who forbade Paul to share what he heard (see Rev 10:4)? Since Paul refuses to provide details, those familiar with Plato and Cicero might have assumed that the apostle's secret vision had something to do with divine mysteries, the future of kingdoms and the end of the world, threats about selfish leaders, and instructions about obtaining lasting glory and life. (Perhaps, they'd be right. It is quite possible these were features of his vision.)

While the context of 2 Corinthians 12 is much different than that of Plato and Cicero's works, all three of them are involved in confronting their opposition. Plato aims to redress the bad theology of the Greek poets, and Cicero contends with the Epicureans' denial of the afterlife. Paul uses his ascent story to counter his agitators too. Rather than quarrelling with heretical poets or rival philosophers, Paul takes on the "super-apostles," who appeal to their own revelations to legitimize their authority to lead Paul's church, presumably away from Paul. In response, the apostle downplays his own revelation to establish the true nature of Christian leadership: humility, service, and grace in the midst of perpetual suffering.

While the super-apostles appeal to stories about their visions for the sake of validation, Plato and Cicero appeal to heavenly ascents to argue for life after death. But here's the kicker: *"Paul does not need his ascent story for that either."* [5] That is to say, over against the super-apostles,

---

[5]Dodson, "The Transcendence of Death," 170.

Paul did not seek legitimacy of his ministry based on *his* being caught up to heaven. It's based on Christ's resurrection from the grave. And, in comparison to Plato and Cicero, Paul's confidence in immortality is also founded on an ascension story—not of Er, Scipio, or even his own—but of the One who rose from the dead and ascended to the right hand of the Supreme God, the author of life. Before Paul had ever been caught up to the third heaven, he had already seen this divine man with his own eyes, high and lifted up, on the road to Damascus (Acts 9:1-6).

FOR FURTHER READING

Primary Sources

Cicero. *The Republic.* Translated by Clinton W. Keyes. LCL. London: Harvard University Press, 1928.

Plato. *The Republic.* Translated by Chris Emlyn-Jones and William Preddy. LCL. London: Harvard University Press, 2013.

Secondary Sources

Blackwell, Ben C., John K. Goodrich, and Jason Maston, eds. *Paul and the Apocalyptic Imagination.* Minneapolis: Fortress, 2016.

Collins, John J. *Seers, Sibyls and Sages in Hellenistic-Roman Judaism.* Leiden: Brill, 2001.

Dodson, Joseph R. "Elements of Apocalyptic Eschatology in Seneca and Paul." In *Paul and the Greco-Roman Philosophical Tradition,* edited by Joseph R. Dodson and Andrew Pitts, 33-54. LNTS. London: Continuum, 2017.

———. "The Transcendence of Death and Heavenly Ascent in the Apocalyptic Paul and the Stoics." In *Paul and the Apocalyptic Imagination,* edited by Ben C. Blackwell, John K. Goodrich, and Jason Maston, 157-76. Minneapolis: Fortress, 2016.

Morray-Jones, C. R. A. "Paradise Revisited (2 Cor 12:1-12): The Jewish Mystical Background of Paul's Apostolate. Part 2: Paul's Heavenly Ascent and its Significance." *HTR* 86, no. 2 (1993): 265-92.

Reynolds, Benjamin E., and Loren T. Stuckenbruck, eds. *The Jewish Apocalyptic Tradition and the Shaping of the New Testament.* Minneapolis: Fortress, 2017.

Stuckenbruck, Loren T. "Posturing 'Apocalyptic' in Pauline Theology." In *The Myth of Rebellious Angels: Studies in Second Temple Judaism and New Testament Texts,* 240-56, WUNT 335. Tübingen: Mohr Siebeck, 2014.

Thrall, Margaret E. *The Second Epistle to the Corinthians.* Vol. 2. ICC. London: T&T Clark, 2004.

Discussion Questions

1. What are the differences and similarities between the accounts of men caught up to paradise in Plato, Cicero, and Paul?

2. How would Plato and Cicero have shaped their reading of Paul's experience in 2 Cor 12:1-8?

3. What, if anything, makes Paul's account unique?

4. As we say above, for some giants of philosophy a righteous person goes straight to heaven when one dies. How do you think Paul would view what immediately happens to us when we die? Compare the philosopher's idea with Paul's (cf. Phil. 1:21-23; 2 Cor 5:1-6; 1 Thess. 4:13-18)?

5. Perhaps the biggest overall difference between Paul's comments and the stories of Er and Scipio is how bereft of details the apostle is in comparison to theirs. Why might this be?

12

IT'S THE HARD-KNOCK LIFE

PAUL AND SENECA ON SUFFERING

BRIAN J. TABB

THE APOSTLE PAUL'S MINISTRY—and his body—was marked by suffering for Christ. In city after city, he was badmouthed, blacklisted, beaten, bound, and booted out of town for proclaiming that Jesus was the crucified Savior and the risen Lord. Yet the apostle rejoiced in his sufferings, boasted in his weaknesses, and stressed that his pains and his chains were for Christ (2 Cor 12:9; Gal 6:17; Phil 1:13; Col 1:24). What was the secret of his joy and contentment in such challenging circumstances? How do his sufferings shed light on the nature and purpose of his ministry?

Paul recounts his toils and trials most extensively in 2 Corinthians 11:23-28, where he contrasts his ministry with that of the false apostles:

> Are they servants of Christ? I am a better one—I am talking like a madman—with far greater labors, far more imprisonments, with countless beatings, and often near death. Five times I received at the hands of the Jews the forty lashes less one. Three times I was beaten with rods. Once I was stoned. Three times I was shipwrecked; a night and a day I was adrift at sea; on frequent journeys, in danger from rivers, danger from robbers, danger from my own people, danger from Gentiles, danger in the city, danger in the wilderness, danger at sea, danger from false brothers; in toil and hardship, through many a sleepless night, in hunger and thirst, often without food, in cold and exposure. (2 Cor 11:23-27 ESV)

Similarly, in 1 Corinthians 4:9-13 and 2 Corinthians 6:3-10, the apostle commends his ministry by highlighting his great endurance, various hardships, and apparent foolishness. These texts have led many to compare Paul's hardship lists with Greco-Roman philosophical writings on suffering.

The Stoic philosopher Seneca, Paul's contemporary, frequently laments his own suffering and the adversities of others. "I am ill; but that is a part of my lot. My slaves have fallen sick, my income has gone off, my house is rickety, I have been assailed by losses, accidents, toil, and fear; this is a common thing" (*Ep.* 96.1). Elsewhere Seneca writes that the wise person may endure destitution, disgrace, public disgust, the death of loved ones, and various other disasters (*Prov.* 4.5-6).

Given that Paul and Seneca discuss the nature and purpose of suffering, we will compare Seneca's *On Providence* with Paul's treatment of his sufferings in 2 Corinthians 11 and other relevant passages.

THE SUFFERING STOIC SAGE

In his essay *On Providence*, Seneca responds to his friend's question about the problem of evil and suffering: "You have asked me, Lucilius, why, if Providence rules the world, it still happens that many evils befall good men" (1.1). Said another way, if a sovereign God exists, why do bad things happen to good people? The Stoic systematically answers this question by considering Providence's true designs, the true nature of hardships, and the true good of the sage.

First, Seneca addresses whether and how "Providence rules the world." The philosopher asserts that his friend's true problem is not belief in the existence of Providence but complaining about its operation (1.4). Seneca likens God (Jupiter) to a glorious parent who severely disciplines his children out of concern for their true good. "He does not make a spoiled pet of a good man; he tests him, hardens him, and fits him for his service" (1.6). This education comes when one is enrolled in the school of suffering. God "tests" people by putting them in the arena so they may demonstrate their true character by facing a formidable foe (3.3). The storm shows a sea captain's skill, and bloody combat proves a warrior's courage (4.4-5). In the same way, adversity uniquely tests and proves one's true character. The good person is "hardened" by experiencing hardship and emerging unscathed and stronger on the other side. Having endured hardships valiantly, the good person is fit to instruct and embody the virtuous life for others (6.2-3).

Second, Seneca clarifies that the calamities commonly considered "evils are not really so" (3.1). Stoics classify all things as good, bad, or indifferent (*Ep.* 117.9). Virtue is good, immoral thoughts and deeds are evil, and everything else—whether one reclines at a banquet or lies on a torture rack—is indifferent or external to one's true happiness or misery (66.18-20). Thus, Seneca rejects Lucilius's claim that "many evils befall good men." Favorable and unfavorable circumstances are not inherently good or evil; rather, people respond to their circumstances by exhibiting virtue or vice (*Prov.* 6.1).

Third, the philosopher urges his friend not to pity a good person who endures hardships, "for he can be called miserable, but he cannot be so" (3.1). This point follows from the previous two in Stoic logic. The philosopher appeals to stock examples of moral virtue, including Rutilius, the committed Stoic who gladly endured exile; Regulus, the Roman war hero who honorably withstood gruesome torture; and Marcus Cato, the fearless general who embodied true Stoic freedom by taking his own life rather than compromising his convictions to wicked rulers (3.4-14). These great people—referred to as Stoic sages—are not unfortunate because they suffered; rather, the fire of adversity revealed their unblemished virtue that is worthy of emulation: "they were born to be a pattern" (6.3). Moreover, while the Stoic God is by nature virtuous and cannot be affected by evil, the sage proves his moral virtue precisely by enduring suffering (6.6). Thus, while it may seem that bad things happen to good people, in truth they don't. Rather, good people learn and show their moral virtue only by enduring and embracing suffering.

THE SUFFERING APOSTLE

Parallels with the Stoic sage. Paul's writings about his own and others' sufferings suggest some conceptual parallels to Seneca's work. For example, the Stoic philosopher would approve of the apostle's appeal for readers to be unmoved by his afflictions (1 Thess 3:3) and his teaching that "suffering produces endurance, and endurance produces character" (Rom 5:3-4 ESV). Moreover, one can picture the Stoic sage saying, "I have learned in whatever situation I am to be content" (Phil 4:11-12 ESV; cf. *On Firmness* 5.4). Seneca would likewise present his fearless hero Marcus Cato taking up Paul's taunt, "Where, O death, is your victory? Where, O death, is your sting?" (1 Cor 15:55 NIV).

Paul's hardship lists share at least five similarities to the nature and purpose of the sage's suffering in Seneca. First, for both writers, afflictions reveal one's moral courage and inner peace. Seneca's wise person is "happy in adversity, peaceful amid the storm" (*Ep.* 41.4), while Paul stresses that he does not lose heart but rejoices in his sufferings (Rom 5:3; 2 Cor 4:16).

Second, people should learn from and imitate those who suffer well. Seneca calls readers to face their fears and imitate the moral courage of great teachers. He considers Cato "the living image of all the virtues," and so he encourages his readers, "Choose therefore a Cato . . . picture him always to yourself as your protector or your pattern" (*On Tranquility of Mind* 16.1; *Ep.* 11.10). Seneca is aware of his own exemplary status and aspires to "find favor among later generations" and "be included among the ideal types of history" (*Ep.* 21.5; 98.13). Similarly, Paul recounts how he has endured persecutions, dishonor, discomfort, and slander and then urges the believers to imitate him (1 Cor 4:16).

Third, adversities are not random but are governed by God's plan (though the Stoic and Christian authors do not mean the same thing by "God"). Seneca calls the good person "God's pupil, his imitator, and true offspring," whom God tests, hardens, and prepares for his service (*Prov.* 1.5-6). Paul writes that "God has exhibited us apostles as last of all, like men sentenced to death" (1 Cor 4:9 ESV) and insists that "for those who love God all things work together for good, for those who are called according to his purpose" (Rom 8:28 ESV).

Fourth, a teacher's exemplary conduct amid hardships demonstrates his personal integrity and the legitimacy of his teaching over against pretenders. Seneca writes, "For we Stoics have declared that these were wise men, because they were unconquered by struggles, were despisers of pleasure, and victors over all terrors" (*On Firmness* 2.1). Paul's sufferings likewise validate him as a genuine apostle and servant of Christ, reveal his sincerity and integrity, and commend his leadership and ministry to the Corinthians (2 Cor 6:3-10; 11:23; Gal 6:17).

Fifth, Paul and the true philosopher are not conquered by adversity but triumph over it. Seneca asserts, "If I am tortured, but bear it bravely, all is well; if I die, but die bravely, it is also well. . . . If I go to the stake, I shall go unbeaten" (*Ep.* 67.15-16). Paul boldly declares that in and through tribulation, distress, persecution, famine, nakedness, danger, and sword, believers "are more than conquerors through him who loved us" (Rom 8:35-37 ESV).

Contrasts with the Stoic sage. But despite the parallels, a careful look at Paul's lists of hardships reveals substantial divergences from Seneca's depiction of the suffering sage. First, for the Stoic, God is "outside of suffering" and admires great souls like Cato whose fortitude in affliction demonstrates that they are "superior" to suffering (*Prov.* 6.6; cf. 2.9). In contrast, Paul declares that the Son of God "humbled himself by becoming obedient to the point of death, even death on a cross," and the apostle longs to "share his sufferings, becoming like him in his death" (Phil 2:8; 3:10 ESV).

Second, the Stoic wise person shows his own self-sufficiency, moral strength, and superior reason when enduring adversity. He is a lonely rock in the sea, constantly beaten by the waves yet unmoved (*On the Happy Life* 27.3). Alternatively, Paul conquers not by his own reason but by Christ's love and power, which is perfected in his weakness (Rom 8:37; 2 Cor 12:9-10). While the Stoic sage is resolute and unaffected by hardships, the apostle acknowledges his weakness, emotional pains, and constant anxiety for the churches (2 Cor 11:28-30).

Third, the philosopher stresses the educational value of hardships, which test, harden, and ready a person to fulfill his or her potential.

The moral exemplars like Cato present a worthy pattern to follow in life and in death, and they teach and encourage people to overcome the fear of death and face the most terrible circumstances with courage (*Prov.* 6.3; *Ep.* 24.9). However, Paul insists that he suffers *for Christ*, to make Christ known. Thus, there is a christological, missiological design to Paul's sufferings. He proclaims a suffering Savior, and he personally portrays the reality of this message by suffering like Jesus (2 Cor 4:10; Gal 3:1; 6:17; Col 1:24-25).

Fourth, Seneca counsels that we should be ready for future suffering but should neither *fear* future calamity nor *hope* for better circumstances (*Ep.* 5.7-9). He calls hope "merely the title of an uncertain blessing" (10.3) and insists that the sage "ever lives happy in the present and unconcerned about the future" (*On the Happy Life* 26.4). In contrast, the apostle's convictions about the future fundamentally shape his perspective on present hardships. He asserts, "the sufferings of this present time are not worth comparing with the glory that is to be revealed to us" (Rom 8:18 ESV). While humanity's basic problem is sin, not suffering, suffering and death came into the world because creation was subjected to futility following humanity's fall into sin (Rom 8:20; cf. Gen 3:17-19). Thus, Paul disagrees with Seneca that suffering is "indifferent." There was no suffering before sin entered the world, and there will be no suffering when God restores all things (Rom 8:21-23). Christians must rejoice and maintain hope amidst present sufferings because God raised Jesus from the dead and will one day raise us with him (Rom 5:2-3; 2 Cor 4:14). Believers experience present suffering followed by future resurrection life, yet we have also been "raised with Christ" (Col 3:1) and are being renewed and transformed daily by his life-giving Spirit (2 Cor 3:18; 4:16; Col 3:10).

CONCLUSION

Paul's hardship lists parallel the catalogues of the sage's sufferings in Seneca's writings in several ways. Paul and Seneca agree that afflictions reveal a person's true character and legitimate his teaching. Moreover, people should not complain about God turning a blind eye to their pain but should remember that God remains in control even when life hurts. Those experiencing suffering should also look to those who have suffered well as worthy models to emulate.

At the same time, the apostle of Jesus Christ and his Stoic contemporary diverge in their emphases about the design of suffering and what suffering shows about human beings and about God. Paul's hardships illuminate the nature and purpose of his ministry as a servant of Christ. The scars on Paul's body and his joy amidst suffering match his message of a suffering Savior who died and rose. He commends himself not through personal eloquence but "by great endurance, in afflictions, hardships, calamities, beatings, [and] imprisonments" (2 Cor 6:4-5 ESV). The apostle's sufferings look to his detractors like weakness and folly, and Paul has a ready answer: a crucified Savior seems foolish and weak according to conventional wisdom, but Christ is "the power of God and the wisdom of God" (1 Cor 1:24 ESV). Similarly, Paul's own apparent folly and weakness reveal the all-sufficient wisdom and power of Christ (2 Cor 12:9).

For Seneca, suffering affords someone an opportunity for moral improvement and self-mastery. The soldier shows he's brave only in the battle, the pilot proves his skill by navigating his ship through the storm, the athlete receives the laurel wreath after competing in the contest (*Prov.* 4.2-5). Cato, Regulus, and other exemplars were not "unfortunate" or "ill-used" because they endured sufferings, sorrows, and premature deaths (3.5-14). These heroes were not victims but victors. By despising death, they showed that they really knew how to live (*Ep.* 77.18). Remarkably, the sage who acquires virtue through suffering, struggle, and study is in some sense morally superior to God, who is virtuous by nature and is exempt from suffering (*Prov.* 6.6; *Ep.* 124.14).

Why do bad things happen to good people if God rules the world? Seneca and Paul would each reframe the question. The philosopher stresses that hardships are not really "bad things" at all but are indifferent to one's true happiness (*Prov.* 3.1). Seen in proper (Stoic) perspective, sufferings are the classroom where the would-be sage learns to be good, as well as the stage where he shows his true virtue. The apostle would respond to Lucilius's question by linking sufferings to Christ, his own apostolic mission, and the inbreaking and anticipation of the age of restoration. Paul would doubtless turn our gaze to the bloody Roman cross where Christ, the only truly good man, suffered willingly to save weak, ungodly people (Rom 5:6-8). He would describe his calling as an apostle of Christ to entail suffering like and for his crucified Lord—the gospel about the death and resurrection of Christ is a gospel he personally embodies. And, lastly, he would explain how sufferings move Christians to rejoice in hope because God will restore all things, as he has already begun to do by raising Jesus from the dead. Those who suffer with Christ now will one day be glorified with him and experience the redemption of their bodies (Rom 8:17, 23).

In the end, the Stoic sage demonstrates his self-mastery in suffering, but the afflicted apostle shows that he is mastered by Christ. Suffering uniquely reveals what people believe, value, and hope for. According to the apostle Paul, suffering Christians should hope and rejoice in God's promises of ultimate redemption and Christ's powerful presence with us in our weakness. When we are weak, we are strong through Christ (2 Cor 12:10).

Table 12.1. Sufferings

The Sufferings of the Stoic Sage	The Sufferings of the Apostle Paul
The suffering sage is morally superior to God, who is unaffected by suffering.	The apostle suffers like and for the Son of God, who suffered for his people.
Sufferings demonstrate the sage's self-sufficiency and superior reason.	Sufferings demonstrate the sufficiency and superiority of Christ, whose power is perfected in human weakness.
Sufferings have an educational design: they test, harden, and prepare people to fulfill their potential.	Sufferings have a missiological design: the apostle's suffering illustrates his message about Christ's cross.
The sage does not fear or hope but is happy in the present regardless of circumstances.	The apostle's hope of resurrection and restoration motivates him to endure and rejoice in present suffering.

For Further Reading

Primary Sources

Seneca. *Moral Epistles*. Translated by Richard M. Gummere. 3 vols. LCL. Cambridge, MA: Harvard University Press, 1917–1925.

———. *Moral Essays*. Translated by John W. Basore. 3 vols. LCL. Cambridge, MA: Harvard University Press, 1928–1935.

Tacitus. *Annals, Books 13–16*. Translated by John Jackson. LCL. Cambridge, MA: Harvard University Press, 1937.

Secondary Sources

Edwards, Catharine. "The Suffering Body: Philosophy and Pain in Seneca's Letters." In *Constructions of the Classical Body*, edited by James I. Porter, 252-68. Ann Arbor: University of Michigan Press, 1999.

Fitzgerald, John T. *Cracks in an Earthen Vessel: An Examination of the Catalogues of Hardships in the Corinthian Correspondence*. SBLDS 99. Atlanta: Scholars Press, 1988.

Hine, Harry M. "Seneca, Stoicism, and the Problem of Moral Evil." In *Ethics and Rhetoric: Classical Essays for Donald Russell on His Seventy-Fifth Birthday*, edited by Harry M. Hine et al., 93-106. Oxford: Oxford University Press, 1995.

Plummer, Robert L. "The Role of Suffering in the Mission of Paul and the Mission of the Church." *SBJT* 17 (2014): 6-19.

Tabb, Brian J. "Paul and Seneca on Suffering." In *Paul and Seneca in Dialogue*, edited by David E. Briones and Joseph Dodson, 88-108, Ancient Philosophical Commentary on the Pauline Writings. Leiden: Brill, 2017.

———. *Suffering in Ancient Worldview: Luke, Seneca, and 4 Maccabees in Dialogue*. LNTS 569. London: Bloomsbury T&T Clark, 2017.

Discussion Questions

1. What similarities and differences between Seneca and Paul did you find most illuminating?

2. How does the philosopher Seneca respond to his friend's question about why bad things happen to good people if God rules the world?

3. Why does Paul call people to hope in times of suffering but Seneca does not?

4. How do Paul's sufferings shed light on the nature and purpose of his ministry?

13

SURPRISED BY PAUL

THE APOSTLE AMONG THE PHILOSOPHERS AND THE POETS

R. DEAN ANDERSON

HAVE YOU EVER BEEN STARTLED TO HEAR a preacher support his or her argument by making a pop culture reference or by quoting a scripture from another religion? If so, this might give you an idea of how some who first heard Paul's speech in Acts 17 were taken aback when he—rather than drawing from Moses, the Psalms, or the Prophets—quoted the pagan poem of Aratus. In Acts 17:28-29, Paul proclaims:

> For "In him [God] we live and move and have our being"; as even some of your own poets have said,
> *"For we too are his offspring."*
> Since we are God's offspring, we ought not to think that the deity is like gold, or silver, or stone, an image formed by the art and imagination of mortals. (Acts 17:28-29 NRSV, italics mine)

While Paul's entire address to the council of the Areopagus (also known as Mars Hill) has been the subject of many books and articles, in this chapter, I wish to focus on this rather startling quotation from Paul in verse 28: "For we too are his offspring."

It helps, however, to know the context of the speech. Luke, the author of Acts, tells us that, while in Athens, Paul met followers of both the Epicurean and the Stoic philosophies there. Even though these were the two most influential schools of philosophy in his day, Stoic philosophy had by far the largest following and the most influence among educated people. And it is this philosophy that Paul clearly plays to in his speech to the Areopagus, where from memory Paul quotes this line out of the introduction of Aratus's Stoic poem the *Phaenomena*.

ARATUS AND HIS *PHAENOMENA*

Aratus spent his student years in the early third century BC among the philosophers and poets in Athens until he was summoned to the Macedonian court in 276 BC. There he was commissioned to write the *Phaenomena*, which aimed to put the learning of the astronomer Eudoxus into poetry so that it could be more accessible and more easily memorized. The poem of some 1154 lines was an immediate success and, particularly in the first centuries BC and AD, became immensely popular. At least twenty-seven commentaries were written on this poem in antiquity.

The *Phaenomena* sets out to give a map of the heavens, the gift of "Father Zeus," and to chart the celestial bodies in order to inform the audience how to organize their daily life accordingly. To get a general idea of the poem, imagine a *New York Times* bestseller that was a mix of a farmer's almanac, a horoscope, and an astronomy book pressed into a poem dedicated to the gods. A real page-turner! Fortunately for those of you disinterested in ancient astronomy, astrology, and math, Paul only quotes from the dedicatory introduction of the *Phaenomena* (lines 1-15, the words Paul quotes are italicized):

> Let us begin with Zeus, whom we men never leave unspoken. Filled with Zeus are all highways and all meeting places of people, filled are the sea and harbours; in all circumstances we are all dependent on Zeus. *For we are also his children*, and he benignly gives helpful signs to men, and rouses people to work, reminding them of their livelihood, tells when the soil is best for oxen and mattocks, and tells when the seasons are right both for planting trees and for sowing every kind of seed. For it was Zeus himself who fixed the signs in the sky, making them into distinct constellations, and organised stars for the year to give the most clearly defined signs of the seasonal round to men, so that everything may grow without fail. That is why men always pay homage to him first and last. (trans. Kidd)

Aratus follows this dedication with a short prayer to Zeus, before the Stoic poet launches into the subject matter at hand. The form of the dedication and prayer follow the general line of didactic poetry from Hesiod. The Zeus described here, however, is not the angry mythological Zeus of Hesiod, but the Stoic Zeus, the Father of humankind who has fixed the stars on the expanse to help and benefit humanity. The older gods recede before this all-pervasive god of the Stoics. This Zeus rules not just the marketplaces (a traditional domain for Zeus), but also the highways (traditionally of Apollo) and the sea (of Poseidon). In contrast to Hesiod's gods, Jews could feel much more comfortable with such a description of the Stoic deity.

ARISTOBULUS AND HIS CITATION OF THE *PHAENOMENA*

In fact, the second-century BC Jewish philosopher Aristobulus[1] also quoted from this section of the poem that Paul would quote a couple of centuries later. Aristobulus, however, conveniently replaces the original "Zeus" with "God" (*Dios* with *Theos*) so that the meter remained intact and the theology cohered with Jewish thought. For Aristobulus, this was a smooth transition, since the sacred verses in the Torah proclaimed that the God of Israel assigned the sun, moon, and stars to the sky to mark the days and seasons for the benefit of humanity (see Gen 1). Aristobulus draws from the poem as part of his apologetic aim to defend the antiquity of the Jews by arguing that Greek philosophers and poets gained their wisdom from the Hebrews.

Since Aristobulus quoted Aratus's introduction centuries before Paul did, the question arises as to whether the apostle is quoting the *Phaenomena* directly in Acts 17 or merely Aristobulus's quotation of

---

[1]Aristobulus, living as a Jewish priest in Egypt (presumably Alexandria), had written a multivolume book dedicated to the boy-king Ptolemy VI Philometor (184–145 BC). Judging by the surviving fragments, it appears to have been an exegesis of passages, mainly from the Pentateuch, set in the form of a dialogue between the boy-king Ptolemy VI and himself. The work can probably be dated to the 170s BC. Analysis of the surviving fragments suggests that Aristobulus was considerably influenced by Stoic philosophy. The claim by Clement of Alexandria that Aristobulus was "Peripatetic" (i.e., Aristotelian) may only be a mistaken derivative from Aristobulus's mention of the "Peripatetic school" in *Fragment* 5.10 (C. R. Holladay, *Fragments from Hellenistic Jewish Authors*, vol. 3: Aristobulus [Atlanta: Scholars Press, 1995], 72).

it. This would be similar to you saying "Money can't buy everything,"
because you often heard it in sermons when you were growing up—
even though you hadn't ever read the essay by Rousseau from which
the saying is drawn. So also, then, it may be that Paul just read the
book of Aristobulus, his fellow-countryman, rather than the original
pagan source. M. J. Edwards has argued that Paul would surely never
have quoted from Aratus in its original form, for this would be tantamount to saying that Zeus, even a Stoic Zeus, is just another name
for the God of Israel. For Edwards, it is more likely that Paul gained
his knowledge of Aratus from the apologetic work of Aristobulus,
who (as we mentioned above) quotes the *Phaenomena* after replacing
"Zeus" with "God."

We can, of course, never know for sure whether Paul gained his
knowledge of Aratus from Aristobulus or from personal acquaintance with the *Phaenomena*. Nevertheless, it is at least just as
probable—if not more so—that Paul quoted Aratus directly. That is
to say, the idea that Paul only knew Aratus through reading Aristobulus seems unlikely. Edwards's chief argument against Paul quoting
Aratus directly is his objection to Paul making use of a poem dedicated to Zeus. But does this fit Paul as we know him? Paul speaks
consciously of his own flexibility in bringing the gospel to people (1
Cor 9:19-23). And the apostle's whole approach to the speech in Acts
17 demonstrates this. Doesn't Paul take his starting point from the
inscription on a pagan altar to an unknown god? It does not seem to
be far-fetched, then, if Paul admits to quoting a thought from their
own poets on the nature of God. In the presentation he is deliberately
using *their* material, not that of the Jewish Scriptures.

Moreover, if you take a stroll through the five surviving fragments
of Aristobulus, you'll find the only real point of connection between
Aristobulus and Paul is the quotation from Aratus. Both authors play
upon the way in which Stoics speak of God. (See Paul's first quote: "in
him we live and move and exist," Acts 17:28 GNT.) However, while
Aristobulus draws from Aratus's poem to conclude that "it has clearly
been demonstrated that the power of God exists through all things"

(author's trans.), Paul uses Aratus to argue against making images of God from gold, silver, or stone.

> Since we are God's offspring, we ought not to think that the deity is like gold, or silver, or stone, an image formed by the art and imagination of mortals. (Acts 17:29 NRSV)

Indeed, in Acts 17:26 Paul has already stated that God "made from one every nation of men" (RSV). Although Paul's words themselves leave the possibility open that he means that God made every nation of men from one nation, as a Jew he clearly means "from one person," and this is also reflected in his quotation from Aratus. When Aratus says that we are the offspring of God, he is distinguishing between God and his creation. This is Paul's point: we ought not to think that the divine being is similar to a tangible image fashioned by man (Acts 17:29). It is therefore clear that Paul is making quite a different point in quoting Aratus than Aristobulus had done.

But was there any incentive for Paul to bother reading Aratus's poem? There is no real theology in it. If he wanted to know about Stoic philosophy he could easily have chosen some other work. It is at this point that we need to remember why this poem was so wildly popular in Paul's day. The ability to read the stars in order to determine when to plant, when to harvest, when to expect storms at sea, and so forth was essential to virtually everybody. Jews were not an exception, and we also see reliance upon recognition of the constellations in the night sky in the Hebrew Bible (see, e.g., Job 9:9; 38:31-32; Amos 5:8). It may have been for very different reasons that Paul originally had studied Aratus (presumably before his conversion). Nevertheless, the line Paul quoted from the dedication came in very handy during his speech to the Areopagus.

PAUL'S QUOTATION OF THE *PHAENOMENA*

Paul's speech to the Areopagus is quite different from his sermons to the Jews in Acts. Although Paul alludes to the Old Testament, there is no quotation from Scripture here on Mars Hill. Nor is there any reference to ancient Israel, a kingdom, a Messiah—let alone biblical figures such as Abraham or David. Paul appears to take things right back to what he considers to be the absolute basics, and then he hooks into the perceived agreements he has with Stoic philosophy. Those unfamiliar with Stoic philosophy might miss these (at least on the surface) points of coherence. The way Stoics spoke of providence and god/Zeus as a caring father for the world could come very close to Jewish (and subsequently Christian) ways of speaking, and Paul plays to this in what he says. The essential difference lies in the fact that, for Stoics, this god was pantheistic. A. A. Long summarizes their position:

> [Stoics] take all phenomena and living beings to be the end observable effects of a cosmic order, constituted and implemented by a principle they called Zeus, God, reason, cause, mind, and fate. This principle, though divine, is not supernatural, but nature itself, as manifested in such different things as the movements of the heavens, the structure of minerals, and the vital properties of plants and animals. Everything that happens is ultimately an expression of this single principle, which by acting on "matter" extends itself throughout the universe and makes it one gigantic organism.[2]

Such a definition did not necessarily, however, prevent prayer to God or the idea that God hears the individual. Zeus was father of all humans and was caring, but this did not exclude pantheism. In other words, the Stoic god does not completely transcend creation. In fact, it was pantheism that enabled Stoics also to speak of gods in the plural and acknowledge the existing system of temples and temple worship, albeit as a symbolic representation of the one divine principle, known as Zeus (cf. Diogenes Laert., 7.147-48). Although not exactly the same, it is similar to the contemporary idea that all religions worship the same God; different people just call him (or her) by different names.

Within his polytheistic context, Paul begins with a typical rhetorical maneuver to capture the goodwill of his audience by complimenting

---

[2] A. A. Long, *Epictetus: A Stoic and Socratic Guide to Life* (Oxford: Oxford University Press, 2002), 20-21.

them on their religiosity. The compliment is, however, capable of double meaning. The atypical word for a Jew, *deisidaimonesterous*, could mean "overly fearful (of the gods)" or "quite religious."[3] The context suggests a positive connotation, but Paul himself may have meant otherwise. Having been accused by some of introducing new gods, he continues by mentioning an altar "to an unknown/ unknowable god." The God he proclaims is therefore not new, but one they already worship, albeit in ignorance. The description that Paul gives of this God is vague enough to have Stoics in essential agreement with him. For Paul, the reference to God "making" the world reflects the account of creation in Genesis 1. However, Paul's use of "make" may simply suggest to a Stoic the notion that the world was "formed" from the eternal elements of earth, water, and heaven to provide for living beings made by Zeus. Indeed, the added notion that God gives life, breath, and all things to all men fits hand in glove with Stoic thinking. Even the argument that God does not dwell in material temples reflects the Stoics' own idea that temples and the worship of other gods pander to the weakness of the masses.

I have already mentioned above that Paul's assertion that all people descend from one person was not typical of Stoic thinking; however, it is precisely this point that Paul backs up with his quotation from the Stoic poem of Aratus. He further uses this quotation as a springboard to the idea that statues of God are completely inappropriate. It is here, however, that Paul departs radically from Stoic thinking. He demands that there be repentance from idolatry and asserts that up until now God has overlooked the times of ignorance, and that a day of judgment is coming. And the proof for this is the resurrection of Jesus Christ. At this point, Luke suggests, the speech was broken off with a measure

---

[3]The translation "superstitious" is often suggested for *deisidaimonia*, but this actually goes too far. The contemporary descriptions of *deisidaimonia* in a negative sense do not suggest superstition. They suggest an attention to minor rituals and gods, which in and of themselves were not out of the ordinary. It is the attention to detail and accumulation of rituals that make one overly fearful of the gods (*deisidaimōn*). Cf. Theophrastus, Char. 16 and the commentary in J. Diggle, *Theophrastus: Characters*, CCTC (Cambridge: Cambridge University Press, 2004).

of mockery. Ridicule is a likely result, since Greeks generally deemed a bodily resurrection both undesirable and impossible.

Paul's rejection stands in stark contrast to Cicero's friend, Cratippus, whom the Areopagus had somewhat recently invited to remain in the city to continue conversing with their young men (Plut., *Cic.* 24.5). Unlike Cratippus, Paul with his "ridiculous" promise of a bodily resurrection received no such invitation. Nevertheless, perhaps as surprising as Paul quoting a Stoic poem, Luke concludes that some from the Areopagus audience joined the apostle and became believers in Jesus Christ. Therefore, Paul may not have won the day in Athens, but he did win some adherents—"including Dionysius the Areopagite and a woman named Damaris, and others with them" (Acts 17:34 NRSV).

CONCLUSION

What we have found investigating Paul among the poets and giants of philosophy in this chapter provides a much more vivid picture of how Paul became all things to all people and how the apostle used any tool he could—even a pagan, Stoic poem—to reach as many people as he could for the gospel. It also shows us an example of how Paul was not the first Jew to use Greek poets and philosophers to illustrate one's respective points. Rather than demonize their poets or discard their philosophies, these two Jews, Aristobulus and Paul, redefined and re-contextualized them. However, *whereas Aristobulus did so as part of an apologetic strategy before the Gentiles to defend the validity of his people and their ancient wisdom, Paul did so from more of an evangelistic agenda.* He used their own poets to persuade the philosophers to put their hope and trust in the one whom God raised from the dead. While for most of the philosophers of Athens, Paul's message would have been considered absolute foolishness, at least some in the Areopagus crowd heard the speech as the good news of salvation, the power and wisdom of God for all who believe—even for philosophers.

For Further Reading

Primary Sources

Holladay, C. R. *Fragments from Hellenistic Jewish Authors*. Vol. 3: *Aristobulus*. Atlanta: Scholars Press, 1995.

Kidd, Douglas. *Aratus: Phaenomena, Edited with an Introduction, Translation and Commentary*. Cambridge: Cambridge University Press, 1997.

Long, A. A., and D. N. Sedley, eds. *The Hellenistic Philosophers*. 2 vols. Cambridge: Cambridge University Press, 1987.

Secondary Sources

Anderson, R. D. *Aratus: Phaenomena (Excerpts) including notes on Acts 17:16-34: A Greek Reader*. Available at http://anderson.modelcrafts.eu/pdfs/Greek/Aratus.pdf (accessed June 15, 2018).

Brunschwig, J., and D. Sedley. "Hellenistic Philosophy." In *The Cambridge Companion to Greek and Roman Philosophy*, edited by D. Sedley, 151-84. Cambridge: Cambridge University Press, 2003.

Edwards, M. J. "Quoting Aratus: Acts 17,28." *ZNW* 83 (1992): 266-69.

Gee, E. *Aratus and the Astronomical Tradition*. Oxford: Oxford University Press, 2013.

Jipp, Joshua. "Does Paul Translate the Gospel in Acts 17:22-31? A Critical Engagement with C. Kavin Rowe's *One True Life*." *Perspectives in Religious Studies* 45.4 (2018): 361-76.

Rowe, C. Kavin. *World Upside Down: Reading Acts in the Graeco-Roman Age*. Oxford: Oxford University Press, 2009.

Sharples, R. W. *Stoics, Epicureans and Sceptics: An Introduction to Hellenistic Philosophy*. London: Routledge, 1996.

Discussion Questions

1. What points in this chapter were new to you?

2. What are some of the places in this passage where Paul differs from Stoic thinking?

3. Is there any area of concern regarding Paul's use of Aratus? Why or why not?

4. What implications does Paul's use of the poem of Aratus have for how Christians engage culture?

14

UNIVERSE TO UNIVERSE

THE CHALLENGE OF COMPARING PAUL WITH THE GIANTS

CHRISTOPHER L. REDMON

"IF YOU WISH TO MAKE AN APPLE PIE from scratch, you must first invent the universe."[1] Thus wrote the late, great astronomer and cosmologist Carl Sagan, who was of course after a truth much deeper than baked sweets. Sagan's point was about human finitude—we make nothing truly "from scratch." Though we may call something like a pie our own "creation," we certainly do not mean that we fashioned it and its ingredients *ex nihilo*. What "creation" turns out to be is instead "reassembly": combining and recombining material in a universe that already contained it.

Sit a bit longer with Sagan's words, though, and we begin to realize a still more profound reality. Indeed, to make an apple pie truly "from scratch," we need not just any universe, but a particular kind of universe with a particular story. We need a universe with the proper elements to constitute an apple, and a universe with the conditions to support botanical life. We need an evolutionary history that produced apples and not some other fruit, and a whole cultural and linguistic world in which "pies" developed as a culinary category. And one could go on. As it turns out, "apple pie" is a remarkably complex thing, tied to the whole physical, biological, and social story that presently gives it meaning. Outside such a story, what we know as "apple pie" would simply not exist.

---

[1]Carl Sagan, *Cosmos* (New York: Random House, 1980), 218.

Sagan's statement, then, is a lesson on just how deeply our lives—
pies and all—are embedded in the world. This is true of both matter
and language. While we like to think of objects and words as concrete,
self-enclosed entities, they are always and everywhere connected to
wider contexts. Objects need a universe in which to be. Words need
a linguistic world in which to operate. Drop a word into a different
world with different rules and a different history, and it will mean
something different—or nothing at all.

So what do pie and the dynamics of language have to do with our
present subject, the intersection of Greco-Roman philosophy with
the life and writings of Paul? Surprisingly plenty. While careful
readers have noted parallels between Paul's literature and the philosophers for centuries, a more recent turn in New Testament scholarship has been to ask whether the philosophers and Paul could fully
understand one another in the first place. Could their vastly different
conceptual "universes" communicate? Could Greco-Roman concepts
be imported into a Christian frame of meaning—or would this be like
rendering "apple pie" into a world without apples? How should we
talk about the influence of Greek philosophy on the Christian tradition, given the complexities of language and life?

The aim of this chapter is not to resolve these questions, but simply
to vouch for their importance and reflect on one scholar's way of
working through them. The scholar in view is C. Kavin Rowe, whose
newest book has raised these issues with regard to Stoicism in particular, and whose proposals deserve the attention of anyone interested in Paul and his philosophical contemporaries.[2] It is up to the
reader to decide whether the arguments, vastly simplified here,
succeed. Even so, they are worth grappling with because of their implications for the whole project of comparative study. What do we
think we are doing, Rowe forces us to stop and think, when we read
Paul next to the philosophers?

---

[2]C. Kavin Rowe, *One True Life: The Stoics and Early Christians as Rival Traditions* (New Haven, CT:
Yale University Press, 2016).

LANGUAGE AND CONTEXT

In a word, Rowe's contribution is about *context*. He invites readers above all to reckon with the dense contexts that ancient philosophies were.[3] This means recognizing what each declared itself to be: the true way of explaining, arranging, and living the totality of life. Put differently, ancient philosophies—Stoicism and Christianity among them—were whole competing universes of thought-and-life, vibrant communities claiming to have the true account of all that is.[4] This, Rowe insists, means something for how we study two philosophies ("traditions") in tandem.

In our analyses of the philosophers and Paul, we often single out particular words or concepts, such as "faith in Romans," "nature in Plato," "the logos in Epictetus," and so forth. While it is surely necessary and often helpful to study ancient figures this way, the approach can also be misleading. Isolate enough words and concepts and we begin to imagine these things as discrete, concrete entities that can be ripped from their wider frameworks without changes in meaning. We may assume that two writers from different traditions who used the same words intended the same things. But did they?

As Rowe sees it, the truth about language is much more complex. Words are not so easily extracted from the wider contexts that give them meaning. In reality, every concept in a tradition like Stoicism or Christianity ("grace," "nature," "God") is always interacting with and deriving meaning from every other, so that the full meaning of one concept is only intelligible in light of the whole arrangement.[5] This

---

[3]Rowe's project focuses on early Christianity and Stoicism, but his findings have implications for how we compare all ancient schools of philosophy. The various philosophical traditions, on Rowe's view, represent competing explanations of the truth, competing accounts of the true way to live.

[4]Rowe draws on the work of philosopher Alasdair MacIntyre for assistance in thinking of Stoicism and Christianity in this way. MacIntyre's word for what both were in the ancient world, which Rowe borrows, is *traditions*. Rowe, *One True Life*, 182-84. See Alasdair MacIntyre, *Three Rival Versions of Moral Inquiry: Encyclopaedia, Genealogy, and Tradition* (Notre Dame, IN: University of Notre Dame Press, 1988).

[5]Rowe is not the first person to make this observation about language. See Samuel Sandmels, "Parallelomania," JBL 81 (1962): 1-13. See also Ludwig Wittgenstein, *Philosophical Investigations*, trans. G. E. M. Anscombe, P. M. S. Hacker, and Joachim Schulte (Malden, MA: Wiley-Blackwell, 2009), 8-22.

makes comparing traditions a challenge, for even when their writers use similar words, the words are embedded in different contexts that lend them ultimately different senses.[6] Consider an example: speech about "death" and "dying" in Paul and Seneca.

"Death" for Paul is not reducible to a simple, universal definition like "the cessation of life." The meaning of "death" is entangled with the whole Christian narrative from beginning to end. It is connected to Paul's story of creation and its subsequent fall and enslavement to evil powers (Rom 5:12-14; 6:20-21; 8:21). It is connected to how Paul talks about sin (Rom 6:7, 16, 21, 23) and to the account he gives of the Torah (Rom 7:1-6, 9-10). It is decisively shaped by its relationship to Israel's God in the crucifixion and resurrection of Jesus (Rom 5:6-8), becoming a defeated enemy that will soon cease to be (Rom 8:38; 1 Cor 15:26, 54-55), and implicating Christian practice (Rom 6:3-4; 1 Cor 11:26; 15:29-32) and practical reasoning (Rom 6:2, 7, 11; 1 Cor 15:56-58) in the meantime. It is finally artificial to think of death as an isolatable *idea* in Paul. It is woven into a dense network of ideas. In the same way that we can't create Sagan's apple pie without first inventing the universe, we can't get at Paul's view of death without summoning his whole narrative world along with it.

"Death" is important also in the writings of Seneca, but there too its meaning depends on the philosopher's overarching story of life. Death, first, is a permanent fixture in Seneca's account of the cosmos.[7] It has no origin or destiny or moral status of its own, but is simply a part of nature's eternal rhythms (*Ep.* 49). Death is therefore intrinsic to what Seneca means by the "human being," so that without exception, humans die (*Ep.* 78.6). Death will accomplish the end of bodily identity as we know it—a kind of return to the existence one had before birth (*Ep.* 54.5)—but it poses no actual threat to the living.[8]

---

[6]Rowe, *One True Life*, 260-61.

[7]By "story," Rowe means something like the narrative underpinning that makes a tradition like Stoicism or Christianity identifiable—and intelligible. See Rowe, *One True Life*, 206-7.

[8]Seneca is happy to entertain the possibility that the soul survives in some vaguer sense that is impossible to discern fully while alive—say, a reintegration into the wider movements of the cosmos (*Ep.* 102.26-27).

Even so, human beings irrationally fear death, which is at the heart of all of their miseries (*Ep.* 4). The fear of death, together with the whims of Fortune that manipulate it, forms habits that bring people terrible distress (*Ep.* 4.7). And yet with proper training, the human being has the resources to overcome its problem with death. A life of Stoic exercises can reframe one's perception so that one is no longer subject to irrational anxieties (*Ep.* 53.9; 61). For Seneca, then, what constitutes freedom is a right orientation toward mortality.[9]

Set side-by-side in their fuller contexts, Paul and Seneca's stories of death come out looking remarkably different. What emerge are two competing accounts in which death has different origins, different destinies, and different implications for a humanity differently understood. Is death an unchangeable fact of life or the defeated enemy of Israel's God? Can bodily identity survive death, or can it not? Is there anything unique about the death of the one person Jesus? What is the problem with death, anyway? Can human beings overcome it on their own? On these points the stories of Paul and Seneca cannot be made to agree. It will therefore not do to think of death as a simple "concept" that Paul and Seneca share, or to imagine that Paul could have moved Seneca's sayings about death into his own framework without basic changes in meaning. The more nuanced approach is to remember how deeply contextualized even the words that Stoics and Christians shared were in the respective universes of each.

KNOWLEDGE AND LIFE

If Christianity and the Greco-Roman philosophies were so contextually dense, how could Paul and a philosopher communicate? Would they have been able to understand one another in conversation if their words meant different things?

Rowe is pessimistic. To be sure, a Stoic or Christian with some patience could attempt to learn the inner workings of the other tradition. She could talk to observers of the tradition and study their texts, doing her best to think with their perspective. But mental effort,

---

[9]Rowe, *One True Life*, 14-21.

says Rowe, can only get a person so far. This is because knowledge in the ancient sense was much more than theoretical—it was practical as well.[10] Knowledge was bound up with lifestyle, so that one had to live in a tradition to learn how that tradition finally thought.

Once more, Seneca and Paul provide examples. Seneca claimed that it would take a lifetime of practice to discover how to live and die as a Stoic (*Brev. Vit.* 7.3). Paradoxically, one had to live *the whole Stoic life* to know what being a Stoic finally meant.[11] So too, Paul thought there were some things that only a practicing Christian could understand. Only by the Spirit, he writes, can sin's corrosive effects on the mind begin to heal; apart from Christ, people reason in darkness (Eph 4:17-24).[12] The Christian life is the process of coming to know the self-revealing God (Eph 1:17-19). This knowledge is inaccessible outside of the lived dynamics of fellowship and faith.

Paul and the Stoics both say, then, that one must join them—and live like them—to understand them. But since no one can live two lives at once, Rowe reasons, no one can understand two traditions simultaneously on the terms they both require.[13] The best one can hope for is an outsider's perception of one as a practitioner of another.

For Rowe, if the claims of Paul and the ancient philosophers to have insider knowledge are true, they directly challenge the habits of modern scholarship. Modern scholars conduct research on the assumption that knowledge is purely theoretical, tacitly rejecting the ancient view that saw knowledge and life in tandem.[14] But if the ancients were correct, and if what we can know is in fact dependent on how we live, we must be considerably humbler in our analyses of philosophies that are not our own. This does not mean that we should stop investigating them. But it does mean that we must be up front about the way that context—including lived, practical context—at last determines what we can say.

---

[10]Rowe, *One True Life*, 235.
[11]Rowe, *One True Life*, 235.
[12]Rowe, *One True Life*, 235.
[13]Rowe, *One True Life*, 245-58.
[14]Rowe, *One True Life*, 243-44.

INFLUENCE AND HISTORY

If Rowe is correct, what does all this mean for how we talk about Greco-Roman influence on early Christianity? Isn't it true that the early Christians knew and borrowed from the philosophers?

Again, says Rowe, things are complicated. We can easily imagine Paul appreciating certain sayings of Seneca were he to have stumbled upon his writings.[15] But Paul would not have appreciated them the way that Seneca did in his own frame of reference. Paul would have appreciated them Christianly, hearing them with the ears of his own tradition and finding them resonant there.[16]

For instance, Paul might well have endorsed Seneca's advice to "weep" but "not wail" at the death of a friend (*Ep.* 63.1). Indeed, Paul wrote to the Thessalonians words that sound similar (1 Thess 4:13). But we should not think that in giving similar advice Paul and Seneca meant essentially the same thing. It was Paul's Christian narrative that gave these words their sense. He could discourage excessive grief because of his firm belief in resurrection: believers will soon reunite with those who have died "in Christ." Seneca, by contrast, was much less interested in schemes of post-mortem survival. Though there is a sense in which the dead are not "lost" but simply precede us in the existence that is everyone's destiny anyway (*Ep.* 63.16), this is hardly tantamount to Paul's hope an of in-person reunion. Seneca's problem with excessive grief is rather that it represents enslavement to the fear of death and to the capricious powers of Fortune that wield it.

Surface similarities, then, betray deep differences. In the end, what Christian-Stoic influence amounts to in Rowe's view is not a clean translation of ideas—as if concepts could be isolated and moved from a Stoic life into a Christian one—but a transformation of words. For Rowe, early Christians found Stoic language resonant in their lives as

---

[15]Later Christians of course did exactly this, imagining a (clearly spurious) *Correspondence* of Paul and Seneca.

[16]Rowe even admits that his own treatment of Stoicism is at best "an account by a Christian who reads as a Christian. . . . I must acknowledge that in practice I am unable to understand certain Stoic things—perhaps even central patterns of reasoning" (*One True Life*, 205).

Christians and claimed it for their own, inevitably reworking its meaning by moving it into a new context of thought and life.[17]

Conclusion

Rowe's work is both stimulating and controversial, but it raises issues the student of early Christianity cannot ignore. He is exactly right to show us the towering complexity of Paul and his philosophical contemporaries. Their lives were more than loose collections of ideas, but were vast integrated wholes, every thought and deed existing in dynamic relationship. It is only fair to our sources to try to honor them as such.

Of course, doing so requires great patience and care. It means avoiding oversimplifications about language and attending again and again to the wider situations of thought and life that give language everywhere its meaning. It means adamantly naming our own contexts too, and becoming more aware of how they have formed us—and might restrict us—as readers. It may even mean admitting that we can never fully grasp another world without first living in it ourselves.

For Further Reading

Hadot, Pierre. *Philosophy as a Way of Life: Spiritual Exercises from Socrates to Foucault.* Edited by Arnold Davidson. Translated by Michael Chase. New York: Blackwell, 1995.

———. *What Is Ancient Philosophy?* Cambridge, MA: Harvard University Press, 2002.

Hays, Richard B. *The Conversion of the Imagination: Paul as Interpreter of Israel's Scripture.* Grand Rapids: Eerdmans, 2005.

———. *The Faith of Jesus Christ: The Narrative Substructure of Galatians 3:1–4:11.* 2nd ed. Grand Rapids: Eerdmans, 2005.

MacIntyre, Alasdair. *Three Rival Versions of Moral Enquiry: Encyclopedia, Genealogy, and Tradition.* Notre Dame, IN: University of Notre Dame Press, 1988.

———. *Whose Justice? Which Rationality?* Notre Dame, IN: University of Notre Dame Press, 1988.

Rowe, C. Kavin. *One True Life: The Stoics and Early Christians as Rival Traditions.* New Haven, CT: Yale University Press, 2016.

---

[17]Rowe, *One True Life*, 260-61.

Sagan, Carl. *Cosmos.* New York: Random House, 1980.

Sandmels, Samuel. "Parallelomania." *JBL* 81 (1962): 1-13.

Stout, Jeffrey. *Ethics After Babel: The Languages of Morals and Their Discontents.* Boston: Beacon, 1988.

Wittgenstein, Ludwig. *Philosophical Investigations.* Translated by G. E. M. Anscombe, P. M. S. Hacker, and Joachim Schulte. Malden, MA: Wiley-Blackwell, 2009.

DISCUSSION QUESTIONS

1. Where do words get their meaning, and what does how we live mean for what we know?

2. What *are* Christianity and the Greco-Roman philosophies?

3. Are there limits to our engagement with other traditions or to the project of comparative study?

4. Given Rowe's fundamental argument, do you think this book is worth reading? Why or why not?

LIST OF CONTRIBUTORS

Justin Reid Allison (PhD, Durham University). Associate Professor of New Testament at Prairie College in Three Hills, Alberta, Canada.

R. Dean Anderson (ThD, Theologische Universiteit Kampen). Reverend of the Free Reformed Church, Rockingham, Western Australia.

Dorothea H. Bertschmann (PhD, Durham University). Honorary Fellow at Durham University in Durham, England, and Tutorial Fellow at the College of the Resurrection in Yorkshire, England.

David E. Briones (PhD, Durham University). Associate Professor of New Testament at Westminster Theological Seminary in Philadelphia, Pennsylvania.

Timothy A. Brookins (PhD, Baylor University). Assistant Professor of Classics and Biblical Studies at Houston Baptist University in Houston, Texas.

Joseph R. Dodson (PhD, University of Aberdeen). Associate Professor of New Testament at Denver Seminary in Denver, Colorado.

Ben C. Dunson (PhD, Durham University). Associate Professor of New Testament at Reformed Theological Seminary in Dallas, Texas.

Nijay K. Gupta (PhD, Durham University). Associate Professor of New Testament at Portland Seminary in Portland, Oregon.

Jeanette Hagen Pifer (PhD, Durham University). Assistant Professor of Biblical and Theological Studies at Biola University in La Mirada, California.

Christopher L. Redmon (PhD Candidate, Duke University).

E. Randolph Richards (PhD, Southwestern Baptist Theological Seminary). Provost at Palm Beach Atlantic University in West Palm Beach, Florida.

Brian J. Tabb (PhD, London School of Theology). Associate Professor of Biblical Studies and Academic Dean at Bethlehem College and Seminary in Minneapolis, Minnesota.

James P. Ware (PhD, Yale University). Associate Professor of Religion at the University of Evansville in Evansville, Indiana.

SCRIPTURE INDEX

ANCIENT WRITINGS INDEX

ANCIENT FIGURES INDEX

ALSO BY JOSEPH R. DODSON

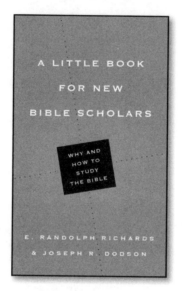

A Little Book for
New Bible Scholars
978-0-8308-5170-6

Finding the Textbook You Need

The IVP Academic Textbook Selector
is an online tool for instantly finding the IVP books
suitable for over 250 courses across 24 disciplines.

---

ivpacademic.com

"Here is a book with a simple yet profound (and much-needed) aim: give people practical ways to take joy in reading the Old Testament and thus help them want to do it more. With pleasing prose and inviting humility, Seibert provides a variety of concrete and creative practices (literary, artistic, theological, and more) that can be adopted by readers at any level. The text's problem parts are addressed (and who better than Seibert to address them?), but with a balanced emphasis on the Old Testament's attractiveness. The end result is a hands-on manual that unlocks access to and stirs affection for an often-neglected part of the Bible. Readers *should* try this at home. They will be glad they did!"

Brad E. Kelle, professor of Old Testament and Hebrew at Point Loma Nazarene University

"Eric Seibert makes reading the Old Testament both fun and practical. Addressing legitimate concerns about problematic portrayals of God, Seibert offers reading strategies that make sense. I plan to give this book to those who think the Bible is boring or irrelevant, because these pages prove otherwise!"

Thomas Jay Oord, author of *The Uncontrolling Love of God* and *God Can't*

"With brilliance, wisdom, and clarity, Eric Seibert shows how to make the Old Testament come alive. Read this book and experience his contagious passion for reading the Bible's first three-quarters. Every professor should make this book required reading!"

Matthew Schlimm, University of Dubuque Theological Seminary

"Professor Seibert's *Enjoying the Old Testament* is a terrific guide for laity and pastors alike. In the tradition of Gordon Fee's *How to Read the Bible for All Its Worth*, this book delivers on its promise to help the reader enjoy what is often seen as the Bible's intimidating and confusing first testament."

Adam Hamilton, pastor and author of *Making Sense of the Bible*

"Many readers of Scripture find the Old Testament boring, legalistic, or ethically troubling. If any of these sentiments are true for you, Seibert's guide will not only enable you to understand the 'Neglected Testament' better, but also to enjoy it—and even love it. The book is filled with wise advice for readers of the Bible as well as helpful, practical suggestions for how to study, learn, and appreciate it. I've been teaching the Old Testament for decades, and my love for it was deepened by his words."

David T. Lamb, MacRae professor of Old Testament and dean of the faculty at Missio Seminary, author of *God Behaving Badly: Is the God of the Old Testament Angry, Sexist and Racist?*